GOD'S DEBRIS

OTHER BOOKS BY SCOTT ADAMS

DILBERT CARTOON BOOKS BY SCOTT ADAMS

GOD'S DEBRIS

A THOUGHT EXPERIMENT

SCOTT ADAMS

**Andrews McMeel
Publishing**

Kansas City

02 03 04 05 RDC 10 9 8 7 6 5

Library of Congress Cataloging-in-Publication Data

Adams, Scott, 1957–
    God's debris : a thought experiment / Scott Adams.
        p. cm.
    ISBN 0-7407-2190-9
    1. Philosophy—Miscellanea. 2. God—Miscellanea. I. Title.
    BD701 .A33 2001
    110—dc21

                                                            2001046100

FOR P.N.O.

AUTHOR'S WEB SITES

Dilbert.com
(*Dilbert* comic strip)

Dilberito.com
(Scott Adams Foods, Inc.)

Staceyscafe.com
(Scott Adams' restaurant)

CONTENTS

CONTENTS

INTRODUCTION

This is not a Dilbert book. It contains no humor. I call it a 132-page thought experiment wrapped in a fictional story. I'll explain the thought experiment part later.

God's Debris doesn't fit into normal publishing cubbyholes. There is even disagreement about whether the material is fiction or nonfiction. I contend that it is fiction because the characters don't exist. Some people contend that it is nonfiction because the opinions and philosophies of the characters might have lasting impact on the reader.

The story contains no violence, no sexual content, and no offensive language. But the ideas expressed by the characters are inappropriate for young minds. People under the age of fourteen should not read it.

The target audience for *God's Debris* is people who enjoy having their brains spun around inside their skulls.

After a certain age most people are uncomfortable with new ideas. That certain age varies by person, but if you're over fifty-five (mentally) you probably won't enjoy this thought experiment. If you're eighty going on thirty-five, you might like it. If you're twenty-three, your odds of liking it are very good.

The story's central character has a view about God that you've probably never heard before. If you think you would be offended by a fictional character's untraditional view of God, please don't read this.

The opinions and philosophies expressed by the characters are not my own, except by coincidence in a few spots not worth mentioning. Please don't write me with passionate explanations of why my views are wrong. You won't discover my opinions by reading my fiction.

The central character in *God's Debris* knows everything. Literally everything. This presented a challenge to me as a writer. When you consider all of the things that can be known, I don't know much. My solution was to create smart-sounding answers using the skeptic's creed:

The simplest explanation is usually right.

My experience tells me that in this complicated world the

simplest explanation is usually dead wrong. But I've noticed that the simplest explanation usually *sounds* right and is far more convincing than any complicated explanation could hope to be. That's good enough for my purposes here.

The simplest-explanation approach turned out to be more provocative than I expected. The simplest explanations for the Big Questions ended up connecting paths that don't normally get connected. The description of reality in *God's Debris* isn't true, as far as I know, but it's oddly compelling. Therein lies the thought experiment:

> Try to figure out what's wrong with the
> simplest explanations.

The central character states a number of scientific "facts." Some of his weirdest statements are consistent with what scientists generally believe. Some of what he says is creative baloney designed to sound true. See if you can tell the difference.

You might love this thought experiment wrapped in a story. Or you might hate it. But you won't easily get it out of your mind. For maximum enjoyment, share *God's Debris* with a smart friend and then discuss it while enjoying a tasty beverage.

THE PACKAGE

The rain made everything sound different—the engine of my delivery van, the traffic as it rolled by on a film of fallen clouds, the occasional dull honk. I didn't have a great job, but it wasn't bad, either. I knew the city so well that I could lose myself in thought and still do the work, still get paid, still have plenty of time for myself. When you're inside your own head, the travel time between buildings evaporates. It's as if I could vanish from one stop and reappear at the next.

My story begins on a day I delivered to a place I'd never been. That's usually a fun challenge. There's a certain satisfaction when you find a new place without using the map. Rookies use maps.

If you work in the city long enough, it begins to deal with you on a personal level. Streets reveal their moods. Sometimes the signal lights love you. Sometimes they fight you. When you're hunting for a new building, you hope the city is on your side. You have to use a little bit of thinking—you might call it the process of elimination—and you need a little bit of instinct, but not too much of either. If you think too hard, you overshoot your target and end up at the Pier or the Tenderloin. If you relax and let the city help, the destination does all the work for you. It was one of those days.

It's amazing how many times you can travel the same route without noticing a particular sign. Then when you're looking for it, there it is. Universe Avenue. I would have sworn it wasn't there a day ago, but I knew it didn't work that way.

It was a scruffy package, barely up to company standards. I calculated the distance from my van to the doorway and decided the packing material could handle the moisture. On behalf of the package and myself, I surrendered to the rain.

This delivery required a signature. Those were the best kind. I could talk to people without any awkward lulls in the conversation. I liked people, but I didn't feel comfortable chatting unless there was a reason. A delivery was a good excuse for some shallow interaction. People were happy to see me and I was never at a loss for words. I'd say, "Sign on this line," and they'd say, "Thank you." We'd exchange some meaningless wishes and I'd be off. That's how it was supposed to work.

I walked up the four steps to the ornate wooden door and pressed the doorbell. A muffled *bing-bong* filled the interior and leaked out the cracks of the doorjamb.

Delivery people don't like to leave the little yellow note, a confession of delivery failure. It means a do-over. I liked to do my work once. I liked my tasks to have beginnings and ends. As a rule of thumb, almost any customer can get to the front door in about a minute. But I usually waited two, in case someone was indisposed or having trouble walking. Two minutes is an eternity when you're standing under a doorway on a rainy San Francisco afternoon.

Rookies wear jackets.

Two minutes passed. The company's rules said I couldn't try the doorknob. They were emphatic about that.

Ah, rules.

THE OLD MAN

The oversized knob offered no resistance as it turned on its oiled core. I was no longer surprised to find unlocked doors in the city. Maybe at some subconscious level we don't believe we need protection from our own species.

I figured I would leave the package inside the door and sign the customer's name. I had signed for customers before; no one had complained yet. It was a firing offense, but that only happened if you got caught.

Inside I could see a long, dark hallway with red faux-textured walls lined with large, illuminated paintings. At the end was a half-opened door to a room that hosted a flickering light. Someone was home and should have heard the doorbell. I didn't like the look of it. Occasionally you read about an elderly person who dies alone and no one knows about it for weeks. My mind went there. I stepped inside and closed the door, enjoying the warmth, deciding what to do next.

"Hello!" I said in my professional voice, hoping it sounded nonthreatening. I shuffled my way down the hall, noticing that the art looked original. Someone had money. Lots.

The source of the uneven light was a huge stone fireplace. I entered the room, not sure why I was being quiet. Somehow the room was both simple and overwhelming. It was half fire-washed color, half black, brilliantly appointed with antique wooden furniture, elaborate patterned walls, and wood floors. My pupils enlarged to tease out the shadows.

An old man's voice rose from the texture. "I've been expecting you."

I was startled and feeling a bit guilty about letting myself in. It took me a minute to locate the source of the voice. It was as if it came from the room itself. Something moved and I noticed, on the far side of the fireplace, in a wooden rocker, a smallish form in a red plaid blanket, looking like a hastily rolled cigar. His tiny wrinkled hands held the blanket like button clasps. Two undersized feet in cloth slippers dangled from the wrap.

"Your door was unlocked," I said, as if that were reason enough to let myself in. "I have a package."

All I heard was the fire. I expected an answer. That's how it's supposed to work. When one person says something, the other is supposed to say something back. The old man wasn't subscribing.

He stared at me and rocked, sizing me up, perhaps, or maybe he was lost in a replay. I had already said what I needed to say, so I stood silently for what seemed too long. I thought I saw the wake of a smile, or maybe it was a muscle tremor. He spoke in the deliberate manner of a man who had not used his voice in days and asked a strange question.

"If you toss a coin a thousand times, how often will it come up heads?"

The elderly are spooky when they degenerate into reflections of their younger selves. They say things that make sense on some grammatical level, but it's not always connected to reality. I remembered my grandfather in his declining years, how he spoke in nonsequiturs. It was best to play along.

"About fifty percent of the time," I answered before changing the subject. "I need a signature for this package."

"Why?"

"Well," I said, measuring how much information to include in my response, "the person who sent the package wants a signature. He needs confirmation that it got delivered."

"I meant why does the coin come up heads fifty percent of the time?"

"I guess that's because the coin weighs about the same on both sides, so there's a fifty-fifty chance it will land on one side versus the other." I tried to avoid sounding condescending. I wasn't sure I succeeded.

"You haven't answered why. You simply listed some facts."

I saw what was going on. The old man pulls this trick question on anyone who comes within range. There had to be a punch line or clever answer, so I played along.

"What's the answer?" I asked with all the artificial interest I could muster.

"The answer," he said, "is that the question has no why."

"You could say that about anything."

"No," he replied, in a manner that seemed suddenly coherent. "Every other question has an answer to why. Only probability is inexplicable."

I waited a moment for the punch line, but it didn't come. "That's it?" I asked.

"It's more than it seems."

"I still need a signature." I approached the old man and held out the clipboard, but he made no motion to take it. I could see him better now. His skin was stained and wrinkled but his eyes were strikingly clear. Some gray hair gathered above each ear and his posture was an ongoing conversation with gravity. He wasn't old. He was ancient.

He gestured to the clipboard with his head. "You can sign it."

In the delivery business we make lots of exceptions for the elderly, so I didn't mind signing for him. I figured his hands or eyes weren't working as well as he liked and I could save him the frustration of working the pen.

I read the name before forging.

Avatar. A–v–a–t–a–r.

"It's for you," he said.

"What's for me?"

"The package."

"I just deliver the packages," I said. "My job is to bring them to you. It's your package."

"No, it's yours."

"Um, okay," I said, planning my exit strategy. I figured I could leave the package in the hallway on the way out. The old man's caretaker would find it.

"What's in the package?" I asked. I hoped to get past an awkward moment.

"It's the answer to your question."

"I wasn't expecting any answers."

"I understand," said the old man.

I didn't know how to respond to that, so I didn't.

He continued, "Let me ask you a simple question: Did you deliver the package or did the package deliver you?"

By then I was a little annoyed with his cleverness, but admittedly engaged. I didn't know the old man's situation, but he wasn't as feeble-minded as I'd first thought. I glanced at my watch. Almost lunchtime. I decided to see where this was heading.

"I delivered the package," I answered. That seemed obvious enough.

"If the package had no address, would you have delivered it here?"

I said no.

"Then you would agree that delivering the package required the participation of the package. The package told you where to go."

"I suppose that's true, in a way. But it's the least important part of the delivery. I did the driving and lifting and moving. That's the important part."

"How can one part be more important if each part is completely necessary?" he asked.

"Look," I said, "I'm holding the package and I'm walking

with it. That's delivering. I'm delivering the package. That's what I do. I'm a package-delivery guy."

"That's one way to look at it. Another way is that both you and the package got here at the same time. And that both of you were necessary. I say the package delivered you."

There was a twisted logic to that interpretation, but I wasn't willing to give in. "The difference is intention. If I leave this package here and go on my way, I think that settles the question of who delivered who."

"Perhaps it would," he said as he turned toward the warmth. "Would you mind throwing another log on the fire?"

I picked out a big one. The retiring embers celebrated its arrival. I had the brief impression that the log was glad to help, to do its part keeping the old man warm. It was a silly thought. I brushed off my hands and turned to leave.

"That chair is yours," he said, gesturing to a wooden rocker next to his. I hadn't noticed the second chair.

The old man's face revealed a life of useful endeavor. I had a sense that he deserved companionship and I was happy to give some. My other choice involved a bag lunch and the back of my truck. Maybe there wasn't any choice at all.

I settled into the rocking chair, letting its rhythm unwind me. It was profoundly relaxing. The room seemed more vivid now and vibrated with the personality of its master. The furniture was obviously designed for comfort. Everything in the room was made of stone or wood or plant, mostly autumn colors. It was as if the room had sprung directly from the earth into the middle of San Francisco.

YOUR FREE WILL

"Do you believe in God?" the old man asked, as if we had known each other forever but had somehow neglected to discuss that one topic. I assumed he wanted reassurance that his departure from this life would be the beginning of something better. I gave a kind answer.

"There has to be a God," I said. "Otherwise, none of us would be here." It wasn't much of a reason, but I figured he didn't need more.

"Do you believe God is omnipotent and that people have free will?" he asked.

"That's standard stuff for God. So, yeah."

"If God is omnipotent, wouldn't he know the future?"

"Sure."

"If God knows what the future holds, then all our choices are already made, aren't they? Free will must be an illusion."

He was clever, but I wasn't going to fall for that trap. "God lets us determine the future ourselves, using our free will," I explained.

"Then you believe God doesn't know the future?"

"I guess not," I admitted. "But he must prefer not knowing."

"So you agree that it would be impossible for God to know the future and grant humans free will?"

"I hadn't thought about it before, but I guess that's right. He must want us to find our own way, so he intentionally tries not to see the future."

"For whose benefit does God withhold his power to determine the future?" he asked.

"Well, it must be for his own benefit, and ours, too," I reasoned. "He wouldn't have to settle for less."

The old man pressed on. "Couldn't God give humans the illusion of free will? We'd be just as happy as if we had actual free will, and God would retain his ability to see the future. Isn't that a better solution for God than the one you suggested?"

"Why would God want to mislead us?"

"If God exists, his motives are certainly unfathomable. No one knows why he grants free will, or why he cares about human souls, or why pain and suffering are necessary parts of life."

"The one thing I know about God's motives is that he must love us, right?" I wasn't convinced of this myself, given all the problems in the world, but I was curious about how he would respond.

"Love? Do you mean love in the way you understand it as a human?"

"Well, not exactly, but basically the same thing. I mean, love is love."

"A brain surgeon would tell you that a specific part of the brain controls the ability to love. If it's damaged, people are incapable of love, incapable of caring about others."

"So?"

"So, isn't it arrogant to think that the love generated by our little brains is the same thing that an omnipotent being experiences? If you were omnipotent, why would you limit yourself to something that could be reproduced by a little clump of neurons?"

I shifted my opinion to better defend it. "We must feel something *similar* to God's type of love, but not the same way God feels it."

"What does it mean to feel something similar to the way God feels? Is that like saying a pebble is similar to the sun because both are round?" he responded.

"Maybe God designed our brains to feel love the same

way he feels it. He could do that if he wanted to."

"So you believe God *wants* things. And he *loves* things, similar to the way humans do. Do you also believe God experiences anger and forgiveness?"

"That's part of the package," I said, committing further to my side of the debate.

"So God has a personality, according to you, and it is similar to what humans experience?"

"I guess so."

"What sort of arrogance assumes God is like people?" he asked.

"Okay, I can accept the idea that God doesn't have a personality exactly like people. Maybe we just assume God has a personality because it's easier to talk about it that way. But the important point is that *something* had to create reality. It's too well-designed to be an accident."

"Are you saying you believe in God because there are no other explanations?" he asked.

"That's a big part of it."

"If a stage magician makes a tiger disappear and you don't know how the trick could be done without real magic, does that make it real magic?"

"That's different. The magician knows how it's done and other magicians know how it's done. Even the magician's assistant knows how it's done. As long as someone knows how it's done, I can feel confident that it isn't real magic. I don't personally need to know how it's done," I said.

"If someone very wise knew how the world was designed without God's hand, could that person convince you that God wasn't involved?"

"In theory, yes. But a person with that much knowledge doesn't exist."

"To be fair, you can only be sure that you don't know whether that person exists or not."

GOD'S FREE WILL

"Does God have free will?" he asked.

"Obviously he does," I said. It was the most confidence I had felt so far in this conversation. "I'll admit there's some ambiguity about whether human beings have free will, but God is omnipotent. Being omnipotent means you can do anything you want. If God didn't have free will, he wouldn't be very omnipotent."

"Indeed. And being omnipotent, God must be able to peer into his own future, to view it in all its perfect detail."

"Yeah, I know. You're going to say that if he sees his own future, then his choices are predetermined. Or, if he can't see the future, then he's not omnipotent."

"Omnipotence is trickier than it seems," he said.

SCIENCE

"I see where you're going with this," I said. "You're an atheist. You think science has the answers and you think religious people are all delusional."

"Let's talk about science for a moment," he replied.

I was relieved. I liked science. It was my favorite subject in school. Religion made me uncomfortable. It's better not to think too much about religion, but science was made for thinking. It was based on facts.

"Do you know a lot about science?" I asked.

"Almost nothing," he said.

I figured this would be a short conversation, and it was just as well because my lunch hour was running out.

"Consider magnets," the old man said. "If you hold two magnets near each other, they are attracted. Yet there is nothing material connecting them."

"Yes there is," I corrected. "There's a magnetic field. You can see it when you do that experiment with the metal shavings on a piece of paper. You hold a magnet under the paper and the shavings all organize along magnetic lines. That's the magnetic field."

"So you have a word for it. It's a 'field,' you say. But you can't get a handful of this thing for which you have a name. You can't fill a container with a magnetic field and take it with you. You can't cut it in pieces. You can't block its power."

"You can't block it? I didn't know that."

"No matter what object you insert between two magnets, their attraction to each other remains exactly the same. This 'field' of yours is strange stuff. We can see its effect, and we can invent a name for it, but it doesn't exist in any physical form. How can something that doesn't exist in physical form have influence over the things that do?"

"Maybe it has physical form but it's small and we can't see it. That's possible. Maybe there are tiny magnetrons or something," I said, making up a word.

"Consider gravity," the old man continued, oblivious to my creative answer. "Gravity is also an unseen force that cannot be blocked by any object. It reaches across the entire universe and connects all things instantly, yet it has no physical form."

"I think Einstein said it was the warping of space-time by massive objects," I said, dredging up a memory of a magazine article I read years ago.

"Indeed, Einstein did say that. And what does that mean?"

"It means that space is bent, so when objects seem to be attracted to each other, it's just that they're traveling in the shortest direction through bent space."

"Can you imagine bent space?" he asked.

"No, but just because I can't imagine it doesn't mean it's not true. You can't argue with Einstein."

He looked away. I figured he was either annoyed at my answer or just resting. It turned out he was pausing to gather energy. He drew a breath into his tiny lungs and began.

"Scientists often invent words to fill the holes in their understanding. These words are meant as conveniences until real understanding can be found. Sometimes understanding comes and the temporary words can be replaced with words that have more meaning. More often, however, the patch words will take on a life of their own and no one will remember that they were only intended to be placeholders.

"For example, some physicists describe gravity in terms of ten dimensions all curled up. But those aren't real words—just placeholders, used to refer to parts of abstract equations. Even if the equations someday prove useful, it would say nothing about the existence of other dimensions. Words such as *dimension* and *field* and *infinity* are nothing more than conveniences for mathematicians and scientists. They are not descriptions of reality, yet we accept them as such because everyone is sure someone else knows what the words mean."

I listened. Rocking, mildly stunned.

"Have you heard of string theory?" he asked.

"Sort of."

"String theory says that all of physical reality—from gravity to magnetism to light—can be explained in one grand theory that involves tiny, string-shaped, vibrating objects. String theory has produced no useful results. It has never been proven by experiment, yet thousands of physicists are dedicating their careers to it on the faith that it smells right."

"Maybe it *is* right." It seemed like my turn to say something.

"Every generation of humans believed it had all the answers it needed, except for a few mysteries they assumed would be solved at any moment. And they all believed their ancestors were simplistic and deluded. What are the odds that you are the first generation of humans who will understand reality?"

"I don't think the odds are bad. Everything has to happen for a first time. You were around to see computers invented and to see space travel. Maybe we'll be the first for this string theory."

"Computers and rocket ships are examples of inventions, not of understanding," he said. "All that is needed to build machines is the knowledge that when one thing happens, another thing happens as a result. It's an accumulation of simple patterns. A dog can learn patterns. There is no 'why' in those examples. We don't understand why electricity travels. We don't know why light travels at a constant speed forever. All we can do is observe and record patterns."

WHERE IS FREE
WILL LOCATED?

"Where is your free will?" the old man asked. "Is it part of your brain, or does it emanate from someplace outside your body and somehow control your actions?"

"A few minutes ago I would have said I knew the answer to that question. But you're making me doubt some of my assumptions."

"Doubting is good," he said. "But tell me where you think free will comes from."

"I'll say it comes from my brain. I mean, it's a function of my brain. I don't have a better answer."

"Your brain is like a machine in many ways, isn't it?" he asked.

It sounded like a trick question, so I gave myself some wiggle room. "The brain isn't exactly like a machine."

"The brain is composed of cells and neurons and chemicals and pathways and electrical activity that all conform to physical laws. When part of your brain is stimulated in one specific way, could it respond any way it wants, or would it always respond in one specific way?"

"There's no way to test that. No one knows."

"Then you believe we can only know things that have been tested?" he asked.

"I'm not saying that."

"Then you're not saying anything, are you?"

It felt that way.

"So where is free will?" he asked again.

"It must involve the soul." I didn't have a better answer.

"Soul? Where is the soul located?"

"It's not located anywhere. It just is."

"Then the soul is not physical in nature, according to you," he said.

"I guess not. Otherwise someone probably would have found physical evidence of it," I said.

"So you believe that the soul, which is not physical, can influence the brain, which *is* physical?"

"I've never thought about it in those terms, but I guess I do believe that."

"Do you believe the soul can influence other physical things, like a car or a watch?"

"No, I think souls only affect brains." I was crawling out on a limb with lead weights strapped to my belt.

"Can your soul influence other people's brains, or does it know which brain is yours?"

"My soul must know which brain is mine, otherwise I'd be influenced by other souls and I wouldn't have free will."

He paused. "Your soul, according to you, knows the difference between your brain and everything else that is not your brain. And it never makes a mistake in that regard. That means your soul has structure and rules, like a machine."

"It must," I agreed.

"If the soul is the source of free will, then it must be weighing alternatives and making decisions."

"That's its job."

"But that's what brains do. Why would you need a soul to do what a brain can do?" he asked.

"Maybe the soul has free will and the brain doesn't," I said. "Or the soul causes your brain to have free will. Or the soul is smarter or more moral than the brain. I don't know." I tried to put my fingers in as many holes as possible.

"If the soul's actions are not controlled by rules, that can only mean the soul acts randomly. On the other hand, if your soul *is* guided by rules, which in turn guide you, then you have no free will. You are programmed. There is no in between; your life is either random or predetermined. Which is it?"

I wasn't prepared to believe I had no control over my own life. "Maybe God is guiding my soul," I said.

"If God is guiding your soul and your soul is guiding your brain, then you are nothing more than a puppet of God. You don't really have free will in that case, do you?"

I tried again. "Maybe God is guiding my soul in a sort of directional way, but it's up to me to figure out the exact steps to take."

"That sounds as if God is giving you some sort of an intelligence test. If you make the right choices, good things happen to your soul. Is that what you're saying?"

"It's not about intelligence, it's about morality," I said.

"Morality?"

"Yes, morality." I felt I was making a good point even though I didn't know what it was.

"Is your brain involved in making moral decisions or do those decisions get made someplace outside your body?" he asked.

I groaned.

GENUINE BELIEF

I needed reinforcements. "Look," I said, "four billion people believe in some sort of God and free will. They can't all be wrong."

"Very few people believe in God," he replied.

I didn't see how he could deny the obvious. "Of course they do. Billions of people believe in God."

The old man leaned toward me, resting a blanketed elbow on the arm of his rocker.

"Four billion people *say* they believe in God, but few genuinely believe. If people believed in God, they would live every minute of their lives in support of that belief. Rich people would give their wealth to the needy. Everyone would be frantic to determine which religion was the true one. No one could be comfortable in the thought that they might have picked the wrong religion and blundered into eternal damnation, or bad reincarnation, or some other unthinkable consequence. People would dedicate their lives to converting others to their religions.

"A belief in God would demand one hundred percent obsessive devotion, influencing every waking moment of this brief life on earth. But your four billion so-called believers do not live their lives in that fashion, except for a few. The majority believe in the usefulness of their beliefs—an earthly and practical utility—but they do not believe in the underlying reality."

I couldn't believe what I was hearing. "If you asked them, they'd say they believe."

"They say that they believe because pretending to believe is necessary to get the benefits of religion. They tell other people that they believe and they do believer-like things, like praying and reading holy books. But they don't do the things that a true believer would do, the things a true believer would *have* to do.

"If you believe a truck is coming toward you, you will jump out of the way. That is belief in the reality of the truck. If you tell people you fear the truck but do nothing to get out of the way, that is not belief in the truck. Likewise, it is not belief to say God exists and then continue sinning and hoarding your wealth while innocent people die of starvation. When belief does not control your most important decisions, it is not belief in the underlying reality, it is belief in the usefulness of believing."

"Are you saying God doesn't exist?" I asked, trying to get to the point.

"I'm saying that people claim to believe in God, but most don't literally believe. They only act as though they believe because there are earthly benefits in doing so. They create a delusion for themselves because it makes them happy."

"So you think only the atheists believe their own belief?" I asked.

"No. Atheists also prefer delusions," he said.

"So according to you, no one believes anything that they say they believe."

"The best any human can do is to pick a delusion that helps him get through the day. This is why people of different religions can generally live in peace. At some level, we all suspect that other people don't believe their own religion any more than we believe ours."

I couldn't accept that. "Maybe the reason we respect other religions is that they all have a core set of beliefs in common. They only differ in the details."

"Jews and Muslims believe that Christ isn't the Son of God," he countered. "If they are right, then Christians are mistaken about the core of their religion. And if the Jews or the Christians or the Muslims have the right religion, then the Hindus and Buddhists who believe in reincarnation are wrong. Would you call those details?"

"I guess not," I confessed.

"At some level of consciousness, everyone knows that the odds of picking the true religion—if such a thing exists—are nil."

ROAD MAPS

I felt like a one-legged man balanced on a high fence. I could keep hopping along looking for an easy way down, or I could just jump now and take my bruises. I decided to jump.

"What's your belief, Mr. Avatar?"

The old man rocked a few times before responding. "Let's say that you and I decide to travel separately to the same place. You have a map that is blue and I have a map that is green. Neither map shows all the possible routes, but both maps show an acceptable—yet different—route to the destination. If we both take our trips and return safely, we would spread the word of our successful maps to others. I would say, with complete conviction, that my green map was perfect, and I might warn people to avoid any other sort of map. You would feel the same conviction about your blue map.

31

"Religions are like different maps whose routes all lead to the collective good of society. Some maps take their followers over rugged terrain. Other maps have easier paths. Some of the travelers of each route will be assigned the job of being the protectors and interpreters of the map. They will teach the young to respect it and be suspicious of other maps."

"Okay," I said, "but who made the maps in the first place?"

"The maps were made by the people who went first and didn't die. The maps that survive are the ones that work," he said.

At last, he had presented a target for me to attack. "Are you saying that all the religions work? What about all the people who have been killed in religious wars?"

"You can't judge the value of a thing by looking only at costs. In many countries, more people die from hospital errors than religious wars, but no one accuses hospitals of being evil. Religious people are happier, they live longer, have fewer accidents, and stay out of trouble compared to nonreligious people. From society's viewpoint, religion works."

DELUSION
GENERATOR

As my lunch hour blurred into afternoon, I had technically abandoned my job. I didn't care. The time spent with this old man was worth it. I didn't agree with everything he was saying, but my mind was more alive than it had been since I was a child. I felt like I had wakened on a strange planet where everything looked familiar but all the rules were different. He was a mystery, but by now I was getting used to his questions that came out of nowhere.

"Has anyone ever advised you to 'be yourself'?"

I said I'd heard that a lot.

"What does it mean to be yourself?" he asked. "If it means to do what you think you ought to do, then you're doing that already. If it means to act like you're exempt from society's influence, that's the worst advice in the world; you would probably stop bathing and wearing clothes. The advice to 'be yourself' is obviously nonsense. But our brains accept this tripe as wisdom because it is more comfortable to believe we have a strategy for life than to believe we have no idea how to behave."

"You make it sound as though our brains are designed to trick us," I said.

"There is more information in one thimble of reality than can be understood by a galaxy of human brains. It is beyond the human brain to understand the world and its environment, so the brain compensates by creating simplified illusions that act as a replacement for understanding. When the illusions work well and the human who subscribes to the illusion survives, those illusions are passed to new generations.

"The human brain is a delusion generator. The delusions are fueled by arrogance—the arrogance that humans are the center of the world, that we alone are endowed with the magical properties of souls and morality and free will and love. We presume that an omnipotent God has a unique interest in our progress and activities while providing all the rest of creation for our playground. We believe that God—because he thinks the same way we do—must be more interested in our lives than in the rocks and trees and plants and animals."

"Well, I don't think rocks would be very interesting to God," I said. "They just sit on the ground and erode."

"You think that way because you are unable to see the storm of activity at the rock's molecular level or the level beneath that, and so on. And you are limited by your perception of time. If you watched a rock your entire life it would never look different. But if you were God and could observe the rock over fifteen billion years as though only a second had passed, the rock would be frantic with activity. It would be shrinking and growing and trading matter with its environment. Its molecules would travel the universe and become a partner to amazing things that we could never imagine. By contrast, the odd collection of molecules that make a human being will stay in that arrangement for less time than it takes the universe to blink. Our arrogance causes us to imagine special value in this temporary collection of molecules. Why do we perceive more spiritual value in the sum of our body parts than on any individual cell in our body? Why don't we hold funerals when skin cells die?"

"That wouldn't be practical," I said. I wasn't sure it was a question meant to be answered, but I wanted to show I was listening.

"Exactly," he agreed. "Practicality rules our perceptions. To survive, our tiny brains need to tame the blizzard of information that threatens to overwhelm us. Our perceptions are wondrously flexible, transforming our worldview automatically and continuously until we find safe harbor in a comfortable delusion.

"To a God not bound by the limits of human practicality, every tiny part of your body would be as action-packed and meaningful as the parts of any rock or tree or bug. And the sum of your parts that form the personality and life we find so special and amazing would seem neither special nor amazing to an omnipotent being.

"It is absurd to define God as omnipotent and then burden him with our own myopic view of the significance of human beings. What could possibly be interesting or important to a God that knows everything, can create anything, can destroy anything. The concept of 'importance' is a human one born out of our need to make choices for survival. An omnipotent being has no need to rank things. To God, nothing in the universe would be more interesting, more worthy, more useful, more threatening, or more important than anything else."

"I still think people are more important to God than animals and plants and dirt. I think that's obvious," I argued.

"What is more important to a car, the steering wheel or the engine?" he asked.

"The engine is more important because without an engine, there is no reason to steer," I reasoned.

"But unless you have both the engine and the steering wheel, the car is useless, isn't it?" he asked.

"Well, yes. I guess that's true," I admitted.

"The steering wheel and the engine are of equal importance. It is a human impulse—composed of equal parts arrogance and instinct—to believe we can rank everything in our environment. Importance is not an intrinsic quality of the universe. It exists only in our delusion-filled minds. I can assure you that humans are not in any form or fashion more important than rocks or steering wheels or engines."

REINCARNATION,
UFOS, AND GOD

I didn't know how much of the old man's opinions to take at face value. Everything he talked about had a kind of logic to it, but so do many things that are nonsense. I decided it was best just to listen. Whatever was happening to me, at least it was different. I liked different.

He started again. "If you want to understand UFOs, reincarnation, and God, do not study UFOs, reincarnation, and God. Study people."

"Are you saying none of those things are real?" I was offended by his certainty, given the thousands of eyewitness accounts for each of those things.

"No," he said, "I am saying that UFOs, reincarnation, and God are all equal in terms of their reality."

"Do you mean equally real or equally imaginary?"

"Your question reveals your bias for a binary world where everything is either real or imaginary. That distinction lies in your perceptions, not in the universe. Your inability to see other possibilities and your lack of vocabulary are your brain's limits, not the universe's."

"There has to be a difference between real and imagined things," I countered. "My truck is real. The Easter Bunny is imagined. Those are different."

"As you sit here, your truck exists for you only in your memory, a place in your mind. The Easter Bunny lives in the same place. They are equal."

"Yes, but I can go out and drive my truck. I can't pet the Easter Bunny."

"Was the rain from this morning real?"

"Of course."

"But you can't see or touch that rain now, can you?"

"No."

"Like the Easter Bunny, the past exists only in your mind," he said. "Likewise, the future exists only in your mind because it has not happened."

"But I can find evidence of the past. I can check with the weather people and confirm that it rained this morning."

"And when you get that confirmation, it would instantly become the past itself. So in effect, you would be using the past, which does not exist, to confirm something else from the past. And if you repeat the process a thousand times, with a thousand different pieces of evidence, together they would still be nothing but impressions of the past supporting other impressions of the past."

"That's just mental gymnastics. You're playing with words," I said.

"An insane person believes his world is consistent. If he believes the government is trying to kill him, he will see ample evidence of his belief in the so-called real world. He will be wrong, but his evidence is no better or worse than your evidence that it rained this morning. Both of you will be converting evidence of the present into impressions stored in your minds and you will both be certain your evidence is solid and irrefutable. Your mind will mold the facts and shape the clues until it all fits."

"That might be true of crazy people, but not normal people."

"Clinical psychologists have proven that ordinary people will alter their memories of the past to make them fit their perceptions. It is the way all normal brains function under ordinary circumstances."

"I didn't know that."

"Now you do," he replied.

GOD'S
MOTIVATION

"If you were God," he said, "what would you want?"

"I don't know. I barely know what *I* want, much less what God wants."

"Imagine that you are omnipotent. You can do anything, create anything, be anything. As soon as you decide you want something, it becomes reality."

I waited, knowing there was more.

He continued. "Does it make sense to think of God as wanting anything? A God would have no emotions, no fears, no desires, no curiosity, no hunger. Those are human shortcomings, not something that would be found in an omnipotent God. What then would motivate God?"

"Maybe it's the challenge, the intellectual stimulation of creating things," I offered.

"Omnipotence means that nothing is a challenge. And what could stimulate the mind of someone who knows everything?"

"You make it sound almost boring to be God. But I guess you'll say boredom is a human feeling."

"Everything that motivates living creatures is based on some weakness or flaw. Hunger motivates animals. Lust motivates animals. Fear and pain motivate animals. A God would have none of those impulses. Humans are driven by all of our animal passions plus loftier-sounding things like self-actualization and creativity and freedom and love. But God would care nothing for those things, or if he cared would already have them in unlimited quantities. None of them would be motivating."

"So what motivates God?" I asked. "Do you have the answer to that question, or are you just yanking my chain?"

"I can conceive of only one challenge for an omnipotent being—the challenge of destroying himself."

"You think God would want to commit suicide?" I asked.

"I'm not saying he wants anything. I'm saying it's the only challenge."

"I think God would prefer to exist than to not exist."

"That's thinking like a human, not like a God. You have a fear of death so you assume God would share your preference. But God would have no fears. Existing would be a choice. And there would be no pain of death, nor feelings of guilt or remorse or loss. Those are human feelings, not God feelings. God could simply choose to discontinue existence."

"There's a logical problem here, according to your way of thinking," I said. "If God knows the future, he already knows if he will choose to end his existence, and he knows if he will succeed at it, so there's no challenge there, either."

"Your thinking is getting clearer," he said. "Yes, he will know the future of his own existence under normal conditions. But would his omnipotence include knowing what happens after he loses his omnipotence, or would his knowledge of the future end at that point?"

"That sounds like a thoroughly unanswerable question. I think you've hit a dead end," I said.

"Maybe. But consider this. A God who knew the answer to that question would indeed know everything and have everything. For that reason he would be unmotivated to do anything or create anything. There would be no purpose to act in any way whatsoever. But a God who had one nagging question—what happens if I cease to exist?—*might* be motivated to find the answer in order to complete his knowledge. And having no fear and no reason to continue existing, he might try it."

"How would we know either way?"

"We have the answer. It is our existence. The fact that we exist is proof that God is motivated to act in some way. And since only the challenge of self-destruction could interest an omnipotent God, it stands to reason that we . . ."

I interrupted the old man in midsentence and stood straight up from the rocker. It felt as if a pulse of energy ran up my spine, compressing my lungs, electrifying my skin, bringing the hairs on the back of my neck to full alert. I moved closer to the fireplace, unable to absorb its heat.

"Are you saying what I think you're saying?" My brain was taking on too much knowledge. There was overflow and I needed to shake off the excess.

The old man looked at nothing and said, "We are God's debris."

GOD'S DEBRIS

"Are you saying that God blew himself to bits and we're what's left?" I asked.

"Not exactly," he replied.

"Then what?"

"The debris consists of two things. First, there are the smallest elements of matter, many levels below the smallest things scientists have identified."

"Smaller than quarks? I don't know what a quark is, but I think it's small."

"Everything is made of some other thing. And those things in turn are made of other things. Over the next hundred years, scientists will uncover layer after layer of building blocks, each smaller than the last. At each layer the differences between types of matter will be fewer. At the lowest layer everything is exactly the same. Matter is uniform. Those are the bits of God."

"What's the second part of the debris?" I asked.

"Probability."

"So you're saying that God—an all-powerful being with a consciousness that extends to all things, across all time—consists of nothing but dust and probability?"

"Don't underestimate it. Probability is an infinitely powerful force. Remember my first question to you, about the coin toss?"

"Yes. You asked why a coin comes up heads half the time."

"Probability is omnipotent and omnipresent. It influences every coin at any time in any place, instantly. It cannot be shielded or altered. We might see randomness in the outcome of an individual coin toss, but as the number of tosses increases, probability has firm control of the outcome. And probability is not limited to coins and dice and slot machines. Probability is the guiding force of everything in the universe, living or nonliving, near or far, big or small, now or anytime."

"It's God's debris," I mumbled, rolling the idea around in both my mouth and mind to see if that helped. It was a fascinating concept, but too strange to embrace on first impression. "You said before that you didn't believe in God. Now you say you do. Which is it?"

"I'm rejecting your overly complicated definition of God—the one that imagines him to have desires and needs and emotions like a human being while possessing infinite power. And I'm rejecting your complicated notion of a fixed reality that the human mind can—by an amazing stroke of luck—grasp."

"You're not rejecting the idea of a fixed reality," I argued. "You're saying the universe is made of God's debris. That's a fixed reality."

"Our language and our minds are too limited to deal with anything but a fixed reality, regardless of whether such a thing exists. The best we can do is to update our delusions to fit the times. We live in an increasingly rational, science-based society. The religious metaphors of the past are no longer comforting. Science is whittling at them from every side. Humanity needs a metaphor that allows God and science to coexist, at least in our minds, for the next thousand years."

"If your God is just a metaphor, why should I care about him? He would be irrelevant," I said.

"Because everything you perceive is a metaphor for something your brain is not equipped to fully understand. God is as real as the clothes you are wearing and the chair you are sitting in. They are all metaphors for something you will never understand."

"That's ridiculous. If everything we perceive is fake, just a metaphor, how do we get anything done?"

"Imagine that you had been raised to believe carrots were potatoes and potatoes were carrots. And imagine you live in a world where everyone knows the truth about these foods except you. When you thought you were eating a potato you were eating a carrot, and vice versa. Assuming you had a balanced diet overall, your delusion about carrots would have no real impact on your life except for your continuous bickering with others about the true nature of carrots and potatoes. Now suppose everyone was wrong and both the carrots and potatoes were entirely different foods. Let's say they were really apples and beets. Would it matter?"

"You lost me. So God is a potato?" I joked.

"Whether you understand the true nature of your food or not, you still have to eat. And in my example it makes little difference if you don't know a carrot from a potato. We can only act on our perceptions, no matter how faulty. The best we can do is to periodically adjust our perceptions—our delusions, if you will—to make them more consistent with our logic and common sense."

GOD'S
CONSCIOUSNESS

"What makes things do what they do?" he asked. "What makes dogs bark, cats purr, plants grow?"

"Before today I would have said evolution makes everything do what it does. Now I don't know what to think."

"Evolution isn't a cause of anything; it's an observation, a way of putting things in categories. Evolution says nothing about causes."

"Evolution seems like a cause to me," I argued. "If it weren't for evolution I'd be a single-celled creature in the bottom of some swamp."

"But what makes evolution happen?" he asked. "Where did all the energy come from and how did it become so organized?"

It was a good question. "I've always wondered how something like a zebra gets created by a bunch of molecules bouncing around the universe. It seems to me that over time the universe should become more screwed up and random, not organized enough to create zebras and light rail systems and chocolate-chip cookies. I mean, if you put a banana in a box and shook it for a trillion years, would the atoms ever assemble themselves into a television set or a squirrel? I guess it's possible if you have enough boxes and bananas, but I have a hard time understanding it."

"Do you have any trouble understanding that a human embryo can only grow into a human adult and never into an apple tree or a pigeon?" he asked.

"I understand that. Humans have different DNA than apple trees or pigeons. But with my banana in the box example, there's no blueprint telling the molecules how to become something else. If the banana particles somehow stick together to become a flashlight or a fur hat, it's a case of amazing luck, not a plan."

"So you believe that DNA is fundamentally different from luck?"

"They're opposites," I said. "DNA is like a specific plan. Probability means anything can happen."

The old man looked at me in that way that said I would soon doubt what I was saying. He didn't disappoint. As usual, he began with a question.

"If the universe were to start over from scratch, and all the conditions that created life were to happen again, would life spring up?"

"Sure," I said, feeling confident again. "If all the things that caused life the first time around were to happen again, the result should be the same. I don't know what you're getting at."

"Let's rewind our imaginary universe fifteen billion years, to long before the time life first appeared. If that universe's origin were identical to our own, would it unfold to become exactly like the world we live in now, including this conversation?"

"I guess so. If it starts out the same and nothing changes it along the way, it should turn out the same." My confidence was evaporating again.

"That's right. Our existence was programmed into the universe from the beginning, guaranteed by the power of probability. The time and place of our existence were flexible, but the outcome was assured because sooner or later life would happen. We would be sitting in these rocking chairs, or ones just like them, having this conversation. You believe that DNA and probability are opposites. But both make specific things happen. DNA runs on a tighter schedule than probability, but in the long run—the extreme long run—probability is just as fixed and certain in its outcome. Probability forces the coin toss to be exactly fifty-fifty at some point, assuming you keep flipping forever. Likewise, probability forced us to exist exactly as we are. Only the timing was in question."

"I have to think about that. It sounds logical but it's weird," I said.

"Think about this," he continued. "As we speak, engineers are building the Internet to link every part of the world in much the same way as a fetus develops a central nervous system. Virtually no one questions the desirability of the Internet. It seems that humans are born with the instinct to create it and embrace it. The instinct of beavers is to build dams; the instinct of humans is to build communication systems."

"I don't think instinct is making us build the Internet. I think people are trying to make money off it. It's just capitalism," I replied.

"Capitalism is only part of it," he countered. "In the 1990s investors threw money at any Internet company that asked for it. Economics went out the window. Rationality can't explain our obsession with the Internet. The need to build the Internet comes from something inside us, something programmed, something we can't resist."

He was right about the Internet being somewhat irrational. I wasn't going to win that debate and this was not a place to jump in. He had a lot more to say.

"Humanity is developing a sort of global eyesight as millions of video cameras on satellites, desktops, and street corners are connected to the Internet. In your lifetime it will be possible to see almost anything on the planet from any computer. And society's intelligence is merging over the Internet, creating, in effect, a global mind that can do vastly more than any individual mind. Eventually everything that is known by one person will be available to all. A decision can be made by the collective mind of humanity and instantly communicated to the body of society.

"In the distant future, humans will learn to control the weather, to manipulate DNA, and to build whole new worlds out of raw matter. There is no logical limit to how much our collective power will grow. A billion years from now, if a visitor from another dimension observed humanity, he might perceive it to be one large entity with a consciousness and purpose, and not a collection of relatively uninteresting individuals."

"Are you saying we're evolving into God?"

"I'm saying we're the building blocks of God, in the early stages of reassembling."

"I think I'd know it if we were part of an omnipotent being," I said.

"Would you? Your skin cells are not aware that they are part of a human being. Skin cells are not equipped for that knowledge. They are equipped to do what they do and nothing more. Likewise, if we humans—and all the plants and animals and dirt and rocks—were components of God, would we have the capacity to know it?"

"So, you're saying God blew himself to bits—I guess that was the Big Bang—and now he's piecing himself back together?" I asked.

"He is discovering the answer to his only question."

"Does God have consciousness yet? Does he know he's reassembling himself?"

"He does. Otherwise you could not have asked the question, and I could not have answered."

PHYSICS OF
GOD-DUST

"If the universe is nothing but dust and probability, how does anything happen?" I asked. "How do you explain gravity and motion? Why doesn't everything stay exactly where it is?"

"I can answer those questions by answering other questions first," he said.

"Okay. Whatever works."

"Science is based on assumptions. Scientists assume that electricity will behave the same tomorrow as today. They assume that the laws of physics that apply on Earth will apply on other planets. Usually the assumptions are right, or close enough to be useful.

"But sometimes assumptions lead us down the wrong path. For example, we assume time is continuous—meaning that between any two moments of time, no matter how brief, is more time. But if that's true, then a minute would last forever because it would contain an infinite number of smaller time slices, and infinity means you never run out."

"That's an old mind trick I learned about in school," I said. "I think it's called Zeno's Paradox, after some old Greek guy who thought it up first."

"And what is the solution?" he asked.

"The solution is that each of the infinite slices of time are infinitely small, so the math works out. You can have continuous time without a minute lasting an eternity."

"Yes, the math does work out. And minutes don't seem to take forever, so we assume Zeno's Paradox is not really a paradox at all. Unfortunately, the solution is wrong. Infinity is a useful tool for math, but it is only a concept. It is not a feature of our physical reality."

"I thought the universe was infinitely large," I replied.

"Most scientists agree that the universe is big, but finite."

"That doesn't make sense. What if I took a rocket to the edge of the universe, then I kept going. Couldn't I keep going forever? Where would I be if not in the universe?"

"You are always part of the universe, by definition. So when your rocket goes beyond the current boundary, the boundary moves with you. You become the outer edge for that direction. But the universe is still a specific size, not infinite."

"Okay, the universe itself might be finite, but all the stuff around it, the nothingness, that's infinite, right?" I asked.

"It is meaningless to say you have an infinite supply of nothing."

"Yeah, I guess so. But let's get back to the subject," I said. "How do you explain Zeno's Paradox?"

"Imagine that everything in existence disappears and then reappears. How much time expires while everything is gone?"

"How should I know? You're the one making up the example. How much?"

"No time passes. It can't because time is a human concept of how things change compared to other things. If everything in the universe disappears, nothing exists to change compared to other things, so there is no time."

"What if everything disappears except for me and my wristwatch?" I asked.

"Then you would experience the passing of time in relation to yourself and to your watch. And when the rest of the universe reappeared you could check on how much time had passed according to your watch. But the people in the rest of the universe would have experienced no time while they were gone. To them, you instantly aged. Their time and your time were not the same because you experienced change and they did not. There is no universal time clock; time differs for every observer."

"Okay, I think I get that. But how is any of this going to answer my original question about gravity and what makes things move?"

"Have you ever seen a graph of something called a probability distribution?" he asked.

"Yes. It has a bunch of dots on it. The places with the most dots are where there's the greatest probability," I said, pleased to remember something from my statistics classes.

"The universe looks a lot like a probability graph. The heaviest concentrations of dots are the galaxies and planets, where the force of gravity seems the strongest. But gravity is not a tugging force. Gravity is the result of probability."

"You lost me."

"Reality has a pulse, a rhythm, for lack of better words. God's dust disappears on one beat and reappears on the next in a new position based on probability. If a bit of God-dust disappears near a large mass, say a planet, then probability will cause it to pop back into existence nearer to the planet on the next beat. Probability is highest when you are near massive objects. Or to put it another way, mass is the physical expression of probability."

"I think I understand that, sort of," I lied.

"If you observed God-dust that was near the Earth it would look like it was being sucked toward the planet. But there is no movement across space in the sense that we understand it. The dust is continuously disappearing in one place and appearing in another, with each new location being nearer the Earth."

"I prefer the current theory of gravity," I said. "Newton and Einstein had it pretty much figured out. The math works with their theories. I'm not so sure about yours."

"The normal formulas for gravity work fine with my description of reality," he replied. "All I've done is add another level of understanding. Newton and Einstein gave us formulas for gravity, but neither man answered the question of why objects seem attracted to each other."

"Einstein did explain it," I said. "Remember, we talked about that? He said space was warped by matter, so what looks like gravity is just objects following the path of warped space."

The old man just looked at me.

"Okay," I said. "I admit I don't know what any of that means. It does sound like nonsense."

"Einstein's language about bent space and my description of God-dust are nothing more than mental models. If they help us deal wth our environment, they are useful. My description of gravity is easier to understand than Einstein's model. In that sense, mine is better."

I chuckled. I had never heard anyone compare himself to Einstein. I was impressed by his cockiness but not convinced. "You haven't explained orbits. Under your theory, how could a moon orbit a planet and not be sucked into it? Your God-dust would pop into existence closer to the planet every time it appeared until it crashed into the surface."

"You are ready for the second law of gravity."

"I guess I am."

"There is one other factor that influences the position of matter when it pops back into existence. That force is inertia, for lack of a better word. Although God-dust is unimaginably small, it has some probability of popping into existence exactly where another piece of God-dust exists. When that happens, one of the particles has to find a new location and alter its probability. To the observer, if one could see such tiny happenings, it looks like the particles collide and then change direction and speed. The new speed is determined by how far from its original spot the God-dust appears with each beat of the universe. If each new location is far from the old spot, we perceive the object to be moving fast."

He continued. "So there is always a dual probability influencing each particle of God-dust. One probability makes all God-dust pop into existence nearer to other God-dust. The other probability is that the dust will appear along a straight line drawn from its past. All apparent motion in the universe is based on those competing probabilities.

"Earth's moon, for example, has a certain probability of coming toward the Earth and a certain probability of moving in a straight line. The two probabilities are, by chance, in balance. If gravity were a tugging force, the way we normally think of it, there would be some sort of friction, slowing the moon and eventually dragging it to Earth. But since gravity is nothing more than probability, there is no friction or tugging. The moon can orbit almost indefinitely because its position is determined by probability, not by tugging or pushing."

"What if all the dust that makes up the moon doesn't reappear near its last position?" I asked. "You said it's only a matter of probability where the dust reappears, so couldn't the moon suddenly vanish if all its dust disappeared and then appeared on the other side of the solar system?"

"Yes, it could. But the probability of that is ridiculously small."

"The trouble with your theory," I said, "is that matter

doesn't pop in and out of existence. Scientists would have noticed that by now."

"Actually, they have. Matter pops into and out of existence all the time. That's what a quantum leap is. You've probably heard the term but didn't know its origin."

"I'll be darned," I said.

FREE WILL
OF A PENNY

"Explain free will," I said.

"Imagine a copper penny that is exactly like an ordinary penny except that for this discussion it has consciousness. It knows it is a coin and it knows that you sometimes flip it. And it knows that no external force dictates whether it comes up heads or tails on any individual flip.

"If the penny's consciousness were like human consciousness, it would analyze the situation and conclude that it had free will. When it wanted to come up heads, and heads was the result, the penny would confirm its belief in its power to choose. When it came up tails instead, it would blame its own lack of commitment, or assume God had a hand in it.

"The imaginary coin would believe that things don't just 'happen' without causes. If nothing external controlled

63

the results of the flips, a reasonable penny would assume that the control came from its own will, influenced perhaps by God's will, assuming it were a religious penny.

"The penny's belief in its own role would be wrong, but the penny's belief in God's role would be right. Probability—the essence of God's power—dictates that the penny must sometimes come up tails even when the penny chooses to be heads."

"But people aren't pennies," I said. "We have brains. And when our brains make choices, we move our arms and legs and mouths to make things happen. The penny has no way to turn its choices into reality, but we do."

"We believe we do," the old man said. "But we also believe in the scientific principle that any specific cause, no matter how complex, must have a specific effect. Therefore, we believe two realities that cannot both be true. If one is true, the other must be false."

"I'm not following you," I said.

"The brain is fundamentally a machine. It's an organic machine with chemical and electrical properties. When an electrical signal is formed, it can only make one specific thing happen. It can't choose to sometimes make you think of a cow and sometimes make you fall in love. That one specific electrical impulse, in the one specific place in your brain, can have one and only one result on your actions."

"We've been through this. Maybe the brain is exempt from the normal rules because of free will or the soul. I know I can't define those things, but you can't rule them out."

"Nothing in life can be ruled out. But the penny analogy is a simple explanation of free will that makes sense and has no undefined concepts."

"Being simpler doesn't make it right," I pointed out. I needed to say something that sounded wise, for my own benefit.

"True, simplicity is not proof of truth. But since we can never understand true reality, if two models both explain the same facts, it is more rational to use the simpler one. It is a matter of convenience."

EVOLUTION

"Let's get back to evolution," I said. "With all your talk about God, do you think he caused evolution? Or did it all happen in a few thousand years like the creationists believe?"

"The theory of evolution is not so much wrong as it is incomplete and useless."

"How can you say it's useless?"

"The theory of evolution leads to no practical invention. It is a concept that has no application."

"Yeah, I hear what you're saying," I said. "But you have to agree that the fossil evidence of earlier species is pretty compelling. There's an obvious change over time from the earlier creatures to the newer ones. How can you ignore that?"

"Imagine that an asteroid lands on Earth and brings with it an exotic bacteria that kills all organic matter on Earth and then dissolves without a trace. A million years later, intelligent aliens discover Earth and study our bones and our possessions, trying to piece together our history. They might notice that all of our cookware—the pots and pans and plates and bowls—all seemed to be related somehow. And the older ones were quite different from the newer ones. The earliest among them were crude bowls, all somewhat similar, generally made of clay or stone. Over time, the bowls evolved into plates and coffee cups and stainless-steel frying pans.

"The aliens would create compelling charts showing how the dishes evolved. The teacup family would look like its own species, related closely to the beer mug and the water glass. An observer who looked at the charts would clearly see a pattern that could not be coincidence. The cause of this dishware evolution would be debated, just as we debate the underlying cause of human evolution, but the observed fact of dishware evolution would not be challenged by the alien scientists. The facts would be clear. Some scientists would be bothered by the lack of intermediate dishware species—say, a frying pan with a beer mug handle—but they would assume it to exist somewhere undiscovered."

"That might be the worst analogy ever made," I said. "You're comparing people to dishes."

The old man laughed out loud for the first time since we began talking. He was genuinely amused.

"It's not an analogy," he said with a twinkle in his eye. "It's a point of view. Evolution is compelling not because of the quality of the evidence but because of the quantity and variety of it. The aliens would have the same dilemma. There would be so much evidence for their theory of dishware evolution that opponents would be mocked. The alien scientists would theorize that forks evolved from spoons, which evolved from knives. Pots evolved from bowls. Dinner plates evolved from cutting boards. The sheer quantity and variety of the data would be overwhelming. Eventually they would stop calling it a theory and consider it a fact. Only a lunatic could publicly doubt the mountain of evidence."

"There's a big difference between dishes and animals," I said. "With dishes, there's no way they can evolve. Logic would tell the aliens that there was no way that a nonliving dish could produce offspring, much less mutant offspring."

"That's not exactly true," he countered. "It could be said that the dishes used human beings in a symbiotic relationship, convincing us through their usefulness to make new dishes. In that way the dishes succeeded in reproducing and evolving. Every species takes advantage of other living things to ensure its survival. That is the normal way living things reproduce.

"You believe, without foundation, that the alien scientists would see a distinction between the living creatures and the nonliving dishes, and classify the dishes as mere tools. But that is a human-centric view of the world. Humans believe that organic things are more important than inorganic things because we are organic. The aliens would have no such bias. To them, the dishes would look like a hardy species that found a way to evolve and reproduce and thrive despite having no organic parts."

"But the dishes have no personalities, no thoughts or emotions or desires," I said.

"Neither does a clam."

"Then why do people say they're as happy as a clam?" I joked. He ignored me.

"Does it strike you as odd that there isn't more evidence today of the mutations that drive evolution?" he asked.

"Like what?"

"Shouldn't we be seeing in today's living creatures the preview of the next million years of evolution? Where are the two-headed humans who will become overlords of the one-headed people, the fish with unidentified organs that will evolve to something useful over the next million years, the

cats who are developing gills? We see some evidence of mutations today, but mostly trivial ones, not the sort of radical
ones there must have been in the past, the sort that became
precursors of brains, eyes, wings, and internal organs.

"And why does evolution seem to move in one direction, from simpler to more complex? Why aren't there any
higher life forms evolving into simpler, hardier creatures? If
mutations happen randomly, you would expect evolution to
work in both directions. But it only works in one, from simple to complex."

He continued. "And why has the number of species on
earth declined for the past million years? The rate of the for-
mation of new species was once faster than the rate of extinc-
tion, but that has reversed. Why? Can it all be explained by
meteors and human intervention?

"And how does the first member of a new species find
someone to breed with? Being a new species means you can
no longer breed with the members of your parents' species.
If mutations are the trigger for evolution, the mutations
must happen regularly and in such similar ways that the
mutants can find each other to breed. You would think we
would notice more mutations if it happens that easily."

"I have the same problem with religion," I said. "It
seemed like there were all sorts of miracles a long time ago

but now we never see them. With evolution, it looks like most of the mutating is petering out just when we get smart enough to study it. It does seem a bit suspicious, as if there was a point to it all and we're nearing it."

"Come back to the coin for a moment," he beckoned. "If by chance you flip a balanced coin and it comes up heads a hundred times in a row, what is the probability that it will come up heads again on the next toss?"

"I know this one. The odds are fifty-fifty, even though it seems like the coin is overdue for a tails. It doesn't make sense to me, but that's what I learned in school."

"That's right," he said. "Or to put it another way, the coin's past has no impact on its future. There is no connection between the outcomes of the prior coin flips and the likelihood of the future ones.

"The rest of the universe is like the coin. The events of the past appear to cause the present, but every time we pop back into existence we are subject to a new set of probabilities. Literally anything can happen."

He shifted in his chair and began again. "Every creature has a tiny probability of becoming a different species with each beat of the universe. A duck can be replaced in whole by a woodchuck. The odds of this happening are so small that it probably never has and never will happen, but it is not precluded by the nature of the universe. It is simply unlikely.

"A more likely result is that a creature's DNA experiences a tiny variation because two bits of God-dust tried to reappear in the same location and had to make an adjustment. That adjustment set in motion a chain reaction of probabilities that affected the fate of the creature.

"When you flip the coin, it almost always lands either heads or tails, even though it could possibly balance on its edge. If we did not have experience with flipping coins we might think coins regularly land and stay on their edges. The edge of a coin has perhaps ten percent as much surface area as either of its sides, so you might expect that coins come up 'edge' routinely.

"But probability avoids in-between conditions. It favors heads or tails. Evolution also avoids in-between conditions. Something in the nature of the God-dust made growing two eyes likely and growing two heads unlikely. More to the point, there is something about eyes that supports God's inevitable reassembly."

SKEPTICS' DISEASE

"I have some friends who are skeptics," I said. "They're in that Skeptics Society. I think they'd tear you apart."

"Skeptics," he said, "suffer from the skeptics' disease—the problem of being right too often."

"How's that bad?" I asked.

"If you are proven to be right a hundred times in a row, no amount of evidence will convince you that you are mistaken in the hundred-and-first case. You will be seduced by your own apparent infallibility. Remember that all scientific experiments are performed by human beings and the results are subject to human interpretation. The human mind is a delusion generator, not a window to truth. Everyone, including skeptics, will generate delusions that match their views. That is how a normal and healthy brain works. Skeptics are not exempt from self-delusion."

"Skeptics know that human perceptions are faulty," I argued. "That's why they have a scientific process and they insist on repeating experiments to see if results are consistent. Their scientific method virtually eliminates subjectivity."

"The scientific approach also makes people think and act in groups," he countered. "They form skeptical societies and create skeptical publications. They breathe each other's fumes and they demonize those who do not share their scientific methods. Because skeptics' views are at odds with the majority of the world, they become emotionally and intellectually isolated. That sort of environment is a recipe for cult thinking and behavior. Skeptics are not exempt from normal human brain functions. It is a human tendency to become what you attack. Skeptics attack irrational thinkers and in the process become irrational."

ESP AND LUCK

"Do you believe in extrasensory perception—ESP?" I asked.

"That depends how you define it," he said. "Skeptics try to make ESP go away by defining it so narrowly that it can't be demonstrated in controlled experiments. Believers hold a more expansive view of ESP, focusing on its utility in daily life."

"So you're a believer?" I prodded.

His expression said no. "There are billions of people on earth. Some of them will have miserable lives from the time they are born until the day they die. Others will have incredibly good fortune in every facet of their lives. They will be born to loving parents in well-to-do homes. Their brains and bodies will be efficient, healthy, and highly capable. They will experience love. They will never be shy or fearful without reason. Some might win lotteries. In a word, they will be lucky over their entire lives, compared to other people.

"Luck conforms to normal probability curves. Most people will have average luck and some people will experience extra good luck or extra bad luck. A handful will have good luck so extraordinary that it will be indistinguishable from magic. The rules of probability guarantee that such people exist."

He continued. "And luck will be compartmentalized in some people, confined to specific areas of their lives. Some people will be extraordinarily lucky gamblers and some people will have amazing business luck or romantic luck.

"Now imagine that you find the one person on earth whose specific type of luck involves the extraordinary ability to guess random things. Such a person is very likely to exist somewhere on earth. What do you think the skeptics would conclude about this person's ESP?"

"If they tested him with controlled experiments and he repeatedly passed, I think they would conclude he had ESP," I said.

"You're wrong. They would conclude that their tests were not adequately controlled and that more study needed to be done. They would say that extraordinary claims require extraordinary proof. And they would keep testing until they either got a negative result or lost interest. No skeptic would take the chance of declaring someone to have

ESP if there were any risk of later being proven wrong. Their cult does not promote that sort of risk.

"To be fair, in all likelihood, the skeptics have never been wrong when debunking claims of alleged extraordinary powers. They believe their methods to be sound because, excluding missteps in individual tests, their methods have never provided a wrong result in the long run, as far as anyone knows. But never being wrong is no proof that the method of testing is sound for all cases."

"Then you think luck is the same as ESP?" I asked.

"I'm saying the results are indistinguishable."

"But it's different because ESP is caused by thoughts traveling through the air or something like that. ESP has to have some cause."

"If you define ESP narrowly to include only the transfer through the air of information, then skeptics will never detect it," he said. "But if you accept luck as being the same as ESP, then ESP exists and it can be useful, though not reliably so, since luck can change in an instant."

"I think scientists have proven that thoughts don't travel through the air because they can't detect anything coming from people's heads when they concentrate," I said, trying to agree. I should have known it would be a waste of time.

"But your thoughts do travel across space," he said. "The question is whether another person can decode the information."

"How do thoughts travel across space?"

"When anything physical moves, it has a gravitational impact on every other object in the universe, instantly and across any distance. That impact is fantastically small, but it is real. When you have a thought, it is coupled with a physical change in your mind that is specific to that thought, and it has an instant gravitational ripple effect throughout the entire universe.

"Can people decode these fantastically weak signals, mixed with an unbelievably large amount of other gravitational noise? No. But the signals are there."

ESP AND PATTERN RECOGNITION

"What about remote viewing?" I asked. "You've heard of that. It's when a psychic draws a picture of some distant place without being there. How's that done? Is that luck too?"

"Sometimes. But pattern recognition is a big part of it too."

"How? There's no pattern if you're sitting in a room in one part of the world and the object is someplace else."

"Everyone has a different ability to recognize patterns in their environment," he said. "It is a skill, like music and math and sports. The rare geniuses in those fields seem downright supernatural. It is as if they possess special powers. In a sense they do, but it would be more accurate to describe their skills as an abundance of a natural ability as opposed to something supernatural.

"Consider a typical math prodigy. Math geniuses often report knowing the answers to problems without being aware of having made a calculation. The top geniuses in every field report the same experience. At the highest levels of performance people are not aware of the processes they are using.

"There is nothing mystical or magical about the performance of geniuses just because they are unaware of how they do what they do. The subconscious calculations of their minds happen so fast that they don't register as memories. It seems as if the answers just arrive.

"Some apparent psychics, the ones who are not intentional frauds, are geniuses at pattern recognition, but they are not necessarily aware of the source of their abilities. Like math geniuses, so-called psychics don't know how they do it. They only know that it works."

"Okay," I said, momentarily accepting his explanation so I could test it. "How does pattern recognition explain a psychic who predicts where a murdered person's body will be found? Where's the pattern?"

"Most of the reports about psychics who locate bodies are false. Reporters usually get their information by talking to people and writing down what they are told, but the stories are only as good as the reliability of the people interviewed. Psychics can make vague predictions and later claim credit for anything that was near the mark. The media tells the story of the fascinating successes and ignores the failures as being not newsworthy. The public gets the impression that psychics can locate dead bodies with regularity. In fact, such cases have been rare and probably a result of genius-level pattern recognition, or luck, or simple exaggeration.

"Let's say the police get a report that a child has been abducted. Police detectives are trained to recognize patterns so they would know that the perpetrator is probably male and probably someone known by the child. And they could predict that the child is dead if missing more than forty-eight hours, with the body probably left outdoors within fifty miles of the crime. Let's say the police call in an FBI profiler who is even more proficient than the police at spotting criminal patterns. Based on experience and statistics with similar crimes, the profiler might predict that the perpetrator has a certain type of background, upbringing, and personality. The police detectives and the FBI profiler can produce information that would seem psychic if you didn't know it was based on simple patterns. Now let's say the police contact a so-called psychic who is a genius at pattern recognition. At the genius level, far more subtle patterns come into play."

He continued. "For example, the entertainment and news media create patterns in the public's minds. Let's say that several movies and TV shows about kidnappings in the past year have created a pattern about the best place to dispose of dead bodies. That pattern could influence a perpetrator to pick a drainage ditch instead of an old shack. The psychic unknowingly picks up on the pattern and 'feels' that the child will be found in a drainage ditch. A search of drainage ditches proves the psychic right.

"In such a case, the so-called psychic's powers would be useful and in some sense genuine, but they could never be reproduced under controlled experiments. In a lab setting, all patterns are removed."

"What about a guy who talks to your dead relatives?" I asked. "He always has information about the survivors and about the dead person that couldn't be a coincidence. How's that done?"

"That, too, is pattern recognition, along with showmanship, and sometimes trickery. Some of what passes as extraordinary psychic ability is nothing but playing the odds. The psychic might say, for example, that the deceased husband saw the widow kissing his picture. That would be a safe guess. Most widows kiss pictures of their dead husbands. Or the psychic might say that the departed husband liked to work with his hands at home. That applies to almost all men.

"The psychic can pick up many patterns suggested from a person's voice, accent, clothes, age, name, health, and ethnicity. Let's say a client has smoke-stained teeth. Smokers are likely to live with other smokers. The psychic might guess that a loved one recently died from heart or lung problems. That would be a good guess."

"Okay, what about those televangelists who heal people on TV? Those people look healed to me. Is that fake?"

The old man just laughed. I laughed too.

LIGHT

"Consider light," the old man said. "Our world appears infused with light's energy. But what is light?"

"It's made of photons," I said, thinking that was a start. By then I should have known better. I think he ignored my answer.

"If you were in a spaceship racing a beam of light, and you were moving at ninety-nine percent the speed of light, how much faster would the light be?"

"About one percent of the speed of light, obviously. I don't know the miles per hour."

"Not according to Einstein. He proved that the light beam would be faster than your rocket ship by the speed of light, no matter how fast you are traveling."

"That doesn't make any sense. But it sounds vaguely familiar. Did he really say that?"

"Yes, and it is accepted as fact in the physics world."

"That's ridiculous," I said. "If I'm traveling ninety-nine percent as fast as the light beam, in the same direction as the light, the light beam can't be faster than me by the same speed as if I weren't moving at all."

"It's ridiculous indeed. But scientists claim it is proven."

"What if two rocket ships were racing the light beam and one was ninety-nine percent as fast as light and the other was fifty percent as fast? The light can't be faster than both of them by exactly the speed of light."

"And yet it would be."

"Okay, that's just plain crazy," I replied. "You see, the light beam should be speeding away from the slower ship faster than it would be pulling away from the fast ship. That's common sense."

"It's common and it's wrong, according to scientific tests," he argued. "It turns out that time and motion and the speed of light are different for all observers. We don't notice it in daily life because the difference is very slight for slow-moving objects. But as you approach the speed of light, the differences become evident.

"It is literally true that no two people share the same reality. Einstein proved that reality is not one fixed state. Instead, it is an infinite number of unique realities, depending on where you are and how fast you are moving.

"If I were a passenger in the slow rocket ship that you used in your example, I would observe you pulling away from me at high speed. But from the perspective of the light beam, neither of us is moving at all. Both versions of reality are verifiably true, yet they are absurd when considered together."

"So what the heck is light?" I asked.

"Light is the outer limit of what is possible. It is not a physical thing; it is a boundary. Scientists agree that light has no mass. By analogy, think of earth's horizon. The horizon is not a physical thing. It is a concept. If you tried to put some horizon in a bucket, you couldn't do it.

"Yet the horizon is observable and understandable. It seems to be physical and it seems to have form and substance. But when you run toward the horizon, no matter how fast you go, it seems to stay ahead of you by the same distance. You can never reach the horizon, no matter how fast you move."

He continued. "Light is analogous to the horizon. It is a boundary that gives the illusion of being a physical thing. Like the horizon, it appears to move away from you at a constant speed no matter how fast you are moving. We observe things that we believe are light, like the searchlight in the night sky, the cloud-red sunset. But those things are not light; they are merely boundaries between different probabilities.

"Consider two plants. One is in direct light and the other is in perpetual shadow. The lighted plant experiences more possibilities because it lives longer and grows bigger and stronger. Eventually it will die, but not before it experiences many more possibilities than its shaded counterpart."

"Okay," I said, "I'm having trouble imagining light as not being a physical thing. How can it influence physical things if it isn't physical itself?"

"There are plenty of nonphysical things that affect the world," he said. "Gravity is not physical, and yet it seems to keep you from floating off the Earth. Probability is not physical, but it influences a coin toss anywhere in the universe. An idea is not physical and it can change civilization."

"I don't think ideas are an example of something non-physical changing civilization. The brains of the people involved are physical things, and they influence our bodies, which are physical. I don't see how ideas really enter into it, except in the way we label things. Ideas don't float around in space by themselves. They're always associated with something physical in our brains."

"Suppose I write a hurtful insult on a piece of paper and hand it to you," he replied. "The note is physical, but when you look at it, the information enters your mind over a pathway of light. Remember that light has no mass. Like magnetic fields, light exists in no physical form. When the insult on the note travels across the light path from the note to your eyes it is completely nonphysical for the duration of the trip. The insult encoded in the light is no more real than a horizon. It is a pure transfer of probability from me to you. When the insult registers in your mind, physical things start to happen. You might get angry and your neck and forehead might get hot. You might even punch me. Light is the messenger of probability, but neither the light nor the message has mass.

"When we feel the warmth of sunlight, we are feeling the effect of increased probabilities and, therefore, increased activity of our skin cells, not the effect of photons striking our skin. Photons have no mass, the scientists tell us. That is another way to say they do not exist except as a concept."

He continued. "You might have heard it said that light is both a particle and a wave, sometimes behaving like one, sometimes like the other, depending on the circumstance. That is like saying sometimes your shadow is long and sometimes it is short. Your shadow is not a physical thing; it is an impression, a perception, left by physical things. It is a boundary, not an object.

"Light can be thought of as zones of probability that surround all things. A star, by virtue of its density, has high probability that two of its God-dust particles will pop into existence in the same location, forcing one of them to adjust, creating a new and frantic probability. That activity, the constant adjusting of location and probability, is what we perceive as energy.

"The reason you cannot catch up to a light beam, no matter how fast you travel, is that the zone of probability moves with you like your shadow. Trying to race light is like trying to run away from your own thoughts.

"The so-called speed of light is simply the limit to how far a particle can pop into existence from its original location. If a particle pops into existence a short distance from its original position, the perceived speed of that particle will be slow. If each new appearance is a great distance from the starting point, the perceived speed will be much faster. There is a practical limit to how far from its original distance a particle is likely to appear. That limit is what gives light an apparent top speed."

"My brain hurts," I said.

CURIOUS BEES

"Why do people have different religions?" I asked. "It seems like the best one would win, eventually, and we'd all believe the same thing."

The old man paused and rocked. He tucked both hands inside his red plaid blanket.

"Imagine that a group of curious bees lands on the outside of a church window. Each bee gazes upon the interior through a different stained glass pane. To one bee, the church's interior is all red. To another it is all yellow, and so on. The bees cannot experience the inside of the church directly; they can only see it. They can never touch the interior or smell it or interact with it in any way. If bees could talk they might argue over the color of the interior. Each bee would stick to his version, not capable of understanding that the other bees were looking through different pieces of stained glass. Nor would they understand the purpose of the church or how it got there or anything about it. The brain of a bee is not capable of such things.

"But these are curious bees. When they don't understand something, they become unsettled and unhappy. In the long run the bees would have to choose between permanent curiosity—an uncomfortable mental state—and delusion. The bees don't like those choices. They would prefer to know the true color of the church's interior and its purpose, but bee brains are not designed for that level of understanding. They must choose from what is possible, either discomfort or self-deception. The bees that choose discomfort will be unpleasant to be around and they will be ostracized. The bees that choose self-deception will band together to reinforce their vision of a red-based interior or yellow-based interior and so on."

"So you're saying we're like dumb bees?" I asked, trying to lighten the mood.

"Worse. We are curious."

WILLPOWER

"You're very fit," the old man observed.

"I work out four times a week."

"When you see an overweight person, what do you think of his willpower?"

"I think he doesn't have much," I said.

"Why do you think that?"

"How hard is it to skip that third bowl of ice cream? I'm in good shape because I exercise and eat right. It's not easy, but I have the willpower. Some people don't."

"If you were starving, could you resist eating?"

"I doubt it. Not for long, anyway."

"But if your belly were full you could resist easily, I assume."

"Sure."

"It sounds as if hunger determines your actions, not so-called willpower."

"No, you picked two extremes: starving and full," I said. "Most of the time I'm in the middle. I can eat a little or eat a lot, but it's up to me."

"Have you ever been very hungry—not starving, just very hungry—and found yourself eating until it hurt?"

"Yes, but on average I don't eat too much. Sometimes I'm busy and I forget to eat for half a day. It all averages out."

"I don't see how willpower enters into your life," he said. "In one case you overeat and in the other case you simply forget to eat. I see no willpower at all."

"I don't overeat every time I eat. Most of the time I have average hunger and I eat average amounts. I'd like to eat more, but I don't. That's willpower."

"And according to you, overweight people have less of this thing you call willpower?" he asked.

"Obviously. Otherwise they'd eat less."

"Isn't it possible that overweight people have the same amount of willpower as you but much greater hunger?"

"I think people have to take responsibility for their own bodies," I replied.

"Take responsibility? It sounds as if you're trying to replace the word *willpower* with two new words in the hope that I will think it's a new thought."

I laughed. He nailed me.

"Okay, just give it to me," I said, knowing there was a more profound thought behind this line of questioning.

"We like to believe that other people have the same level of urges as we do, despite all evidence to the contrary. We convince ourselves that people differ only in their degree of morality or willpower, or a combination of the two. But urges are real, and they differ wildly for every individual. Morality and willpower are illusions. For any human being, the highest urge always wins and willpower never enters into it. Willpower is a delusion."

"Your interpretation is dangerous," I said. "You're saying it's okay to follow your urges, no matter what is right or wrong, because you can't help yourself anyway. We might as well empty the prisons since people can't stop themselves from committing crimes. It's not really their fault, according to you."

"It is useful to society that our urges are tempered by shame and condemnation and the threat of punishment," he said. "It is a useful fiction to blame a thing called willpower and pretend the individual is somehow capable of overcoming urges with this magical and invisible force. Without that fiction, there could be no blame, no indignation, and no universal agreement that some things should be punished. And without those very real limiting forces, our urges would be less contained and more disruptive than they are. The delusion of willpower is a practical fiction."

"I'll never look at pie the same way," I said. "But what about people with slow metabolisms? They get fat no matter how little they eat."

"Have you ever seen pictures of starving people?" he asked.

"Yes."

"How many of the starving people in those pictures were fat?"

"None that I've seen. They're always skin and bones. But that's different."

"It's very different but still, according to your theory, some of those people should be starving to death while remaining fat."

I didn't have an answer for that. I was happy when he changed the subject.

HOLY LANDS

"What makes a holy land holy?" he asked.

"Well, usually it's because some important religious event took place there."

"What does it mean to say that something took place in a particular location when we know that the earth is constantly in motion, rotating on its axis and orbiting the sun? And we're in a moving galaxy that is part of an expanding universe. Even if you had a spaceship and could fly anywhere, you can never return to the location of a past event. There would be no equivalent of the past location because location depends on your distance from other objects, and all objects in the universe would have moved considerably by then."

"I see your point, but on Earth the holy places keep their relationship to other things on Earth, and those things don't move much," I said.

"Let's say you dug up all the dirt and rocks and vegetation of a holy place and moved it someplace else, leaving nothing but a hole that is one mile deep in the original location. Would the holy land now be the new location where you put the dirt and rocks and vegetation, or the old location with the hole?"

"I think both would be considered holy," I said, hedging my bets.

"Suppose you took only the very top layer of soil and vegetation from the holy place, the newer stuff that blew in or grew after the religious event occurred thousands of years ago. Would the place you dumped the topsoil and vegetation be holy?"

"That's a little trickier," I said. "I'll say the new location isn't holy because the topsoil that you moved there isn't itself holy, it was only in contact with holy land. If holy land could turn anything that touched it into more holy land, then the whole planet would be holy."

The old man smiled. "The concept of location is a useful delusion when applied to real estate ownership, or when giving someone directions to the store. But when it is viewed through the eyes of an omnipotent God, the concept of location is absurd.

"While we speak, nations are arming themselves to fight

for control of lands they consider holy. They are trapped in the delusion that locations are real things, not just fictions of the mind. Many will die."

FIGHTING GOD

"So what good is all this?" I asked. "Let's say you convinced me that probability is the best way to understand the universe and that probability is the essence of God. How does that help me? Should I pray to this God of yours? Do I need to satisfy him in some way?"

"Probability is the expression of God's will. It is in your best interest to obey probability."

"How do I obey probability?"

"God's reassembly requires people—living, healthy people," he said. "When you buckle your seat belt, you increase your chances of living. That is obeying probability. If you get drunk and drive without a seat belt, you are fighting probability."

"I don't see how I'm helping God's reassembly," I said. "I just deliver packages. I'm not designing the Internet or anything."

"Every economic activity helps. Whether you are programming computers, or growing food, or raising children, or cleaning garbage from the side of the road, you are contributing to the realization of God's consciousness. None of those activities is more important than another."

"What about good and evil? Do they exist in your model?" I asked.

"Evil is any action that might damage people. Probability generally punishes evildoers. Since most criminals are captured and jailed, overall the people who hurt others tend to pay. So evil does exist and, on average, it is punished.

"Life has a feel and flow to it. Usually you know instinctively when you are working with probability on your side and when you are fighting it. When you take your education seriously, for example, you are greatly increasing your probability of contributing to God's reassembly. When you love and respect others and procreate responsibly, you are living within the safety cone of probability. You are, in a sense, fulfilling God's will."

"That sounds like karma," I said. "When you do good things, good things come back to you."

"Yes, but good things do not return in a one-for-one manner. Individual actions are not directly rewarded. It is only on average that doing good improves the quality of life for you and the people around you."

"Does God forgive people, in a manner of speaking?"

"Yes, essentially, by exerting control over the averages of human activity and not the individual acts. Every person has the opportunity to improve his average contribution to society regardless of what he has done in the past."

"What about an afterlife? Where's the payoff? What difference does it make to me whether I contribute to society or not? I'll die anyway, eventually. Why should I care if God gets conscious or not?" I asked.

"God will become conscious whether you as an individual are in harmony with probability or not. God controls the averages, not the individuals. Your short-term payoff for contributing to God's consciousness is fewer problems in your daily life, less stress, and more happiness.

"Stress is the cause of all unhappiness and it comes in infinite varieties, all with a common cause. Stress is a result of fighting probability, and the friction between what you are doing and what you know you should be doing to live within probability."

"That sounds simplistic," I said. "Sometimes stress just happens to you because you're in the wrong place at the wrong time. Let's say a family member dies of old age. That's stressful but there's nothing you could do about it."

"Stress cannot be eliminated from your life. But you can reduce stress by being in harmony with probability. You can deal with the death of a loved one more easily if you have done proper estate planning and are mentally prepared for the inevitable. If you have been a good friend to many people and stayed close to your family, the loss will be softened. If you allow your mind to release the past instead of trying to wish the deceased back to life, or wishing you had done something different, then your stress will be less."

"What about the afterlife? Are all the benefits here and now or is there something later?" I asked.

"Over time, everything that is possible happens. That is a fundamental quality of probability. If you flip a coin often enough, eventually it will come up heads a thousand times in a row. And everything possible will happen over and over as long as God's debris exists. The clump of debris that comprises your body and mind will break down and disintegrate someday, but a version of you will reappear in the future, by chance."

"Are you saying I'll reincarnate?"

"Not exactly. I'm saying a replica of your mind and body will exist in the distant future, by chance. And the things you do now can either make life more pleasant or more difficult for your replica."

"Why would I care about a replica of me? That's a different guy."

"That distinction is an illusion. In your current life, every cell in your body has died and been replaced many times. There is nothing in your current body that you were born with. You have no original equipment, just replacement parts, so for all practical purposes, you are already a replica of a prior version of you."

"Yes, but my memories stay with me. The replica of me in the distant future will have none of the memories and feelings that comprise my life," I said.

"There will be many replicas of you in the future, not just one. Some will have lives similar to yours, with similar memories and feelings. The replicas will be different from you only in concept, not in practical terms."

"The thing I like about your view of God is that it's easy to follow the rules. All I have to do is go with probability."

"Sometimes it is easy," he said. "Other times it will be hard to sort out the right probabilities. Today, the news reported that teens who publicly commit to avoiding sex have more success in abstaining, compared to those who don't. What would you conclude about the probabilities in that story?"

"Obviously it helps to make the public commitment. That improves your odds."

"Perhaps. Or maybe the teens who wanted to abstain

were the only ones who were willing to publicly commit. Or maybe the teens who made the public commitments were more likely to later lie about their rate of sex. Probability is simple but it is not always obvious."

RELATIONSHIPS

The old man rocked some more and smiled at me. "You're alone much of the time."

He was right. I enjoyed being alone. I had friends, but I was always happy to get back home.

"How do you know that?" I asked.

"Your pupils widen when I talk about ideas."

"They do?"

"There are two types of people in the world, my young friend. One type is people-oriented. When they make conversation, it is about people—what people are doing, what someone said, how someone feels. The other group is idea-oriented. When they make conversation, they talk about ideas and concepts and objects."

"I must be an idea person."

"Yes. And it causes trouble in your personal life but you don't realize how."

"That's rather presumptuous of you. What makes you think I have trouble in my personal life?" I had to admit he was right. Everyone has an imperfect personal life, but for me that imperfection was almost a defining principle.

He continued, "Idea people like you are boring, even to other idea people."

"Hey, I'm insulted," I said, not really feeling so. "I will admit I'm not the life of any party. Whenever I try to inject something interesting into a conversation everyone gets quiet until someone changes the topic. I think I'm pretty interesting but no one else does. All of the popular people seem to babble about nothing, but I usually have something interesting to say. You'd think people would like that."

"Actually, the popular people only *seem* to be babbling," he countered. "In fact, they talk about a topic that everyone cares about; they talk about people. When a person talks about people, it is personal to everyone who listens. You will automatically relate the story to yourself, thinking how you would react in that person's situation, how your life has parallels. On the other hand, if you tell a story about a new type of tool you found at the hardware store, no one can relate to the tool on a personal level. It is just an object, no matter how useful or novel."

"Okay, so how do I become more interesting?"

"If I gave you advice, would you follow it?"

"Maybe. It depends on the advice."

"No, you wouldn't follow my advice. No one has ever followed the advice of another person."

"Now you're just being disagreeable," I said. "Obviously people follow advice all the time. That's not a delusion."

"People think they follow advice but they don't. Humans are only capable of receiving information. They create their own advice. If you seek to influence someone, don't waste time giving advice. You can change only what people know, not what they do."

"Okay then. Can you give me some information that would help my personal life?"

"Perhaps," he said, clenching his red plaid blanket tighter around his tiny body. "What topic interests you more than any other?"

"Myself, I guess," I confessed.

"Yes, that is the essence of being human. Any person you meet at a party will be interested in his own life above all other topics. Your awkward silences can be solved by asking simple questions about the person's life."

"That would be totally phony," I said. "First of all, it would be like interrogating him. Secondly, I couldn't possibly pretend to be interested in the answers. If he turns out to be some shoe salesman living with his mother in Albany, my eyes will glaze over."

"It would seem phony to you while you asked the questions, but it would not seem that way to the stranger. To him it is an unexpected gift, an opportunity to enjoy one of life's greatest pleasures: talking about oneself. He would become more animated and he would instantly begin to like you. You would seem to be a brilliant and talented conversationalist, even if your only contribution was asking questions and listening. And you would have solved the stranger's fear of an awkward silence. For that he will be grateful."

"That solves the stranger's problem, but I have to listen to this guy drone on about himself. The cure is worse than the disease."

"Your questions to the stranger are only the starting points. From there you can steer him toward the thing you care about most—yourself."

"Wouldn't he want to talk about himself instead of me?"

"When you find out how others deal with their situations it is automatically relevant to you," he said. "There will always be parallels in your life. Find out what you and he have in common, then ask how he likes it, how he deals with it, and if he has any clever solutions for it. Perhaps you both have long commutes, or you both have mothers who call too often or you both ski. Find that point of common interest and you will both be talking about yourself to the delight of the other."

"What about sharing my opinions on important things?" I asked. "I'm always getting into debates with people. It seems like I always have a more thought-out view of things and I feel like I have a responsibility to set people straight. Sometimes, though, I wish I could just shut up. But when you hear the crazy views that some people have—actually, most people—how can you just let it slide?"

"Have you ever been in traffic behind someone who doesn't move when the light turns green, so you honk your horn, then you realize the car is stalled and there is nothing the driver could have done?"

"Yeah, I've honked. It's embarrassing," I said.

"Most disagreements are like my example. Two people have different information, but they think the root of their disagreement is that the other person has bad judgment or bad manners or bad values. In fact, most people would share your opinions if they had the same information. If you spend your time arguing about the faultiness of other people's opinions, you waste your time and theirs. The only thing than can be useful is examining the differences in your assumptions and adding to each other's information. Sometimes that is enough to make viewpoints converge over time."

"Hey, if you can teach me to get along with women, I could sure use that."

"I can tell you some things."

"I'll take whatever help I can get."

"Women believe that men are, in a sense, defective versions of women," he began. "Men believe that women are defective versions of men. Both genders are trapped in a delusion that their personal viewpoints are universal. That viewpoint—that each gender is a defective version of the other—is the root of all misunderstandings."

"How does that help me?" I asked.

"Women define themselves by their relationships and men define themselves by whom they are helping. Women believe value is created by sacrifice. If you are willing to give up your favorite activities to be with her, she will trust you. If being with her is too easy for you, she will not trust you. You can accomplish your sacrifices symbolically at first, by leaving work early to buy flowers, canceling your softball game to make a date, that sort of thing."

"Why does it seem like the rich and famous guys get all the women?" I asked.

"Partly because the rich and famous are capable of making larger sacrifices. The average man might be sacrificing a night of television to be with a woman. The rich and famous man could be sacrificing a week in Tahiti. There is much to be said about the attraction of power and confidence exuded by a rich and powerful man, but capacity for sacrifice is the most important thing."

"What do men value?" I asked.

"Men believe value is created by accomplishment, and they have objectives for the women in their lives. If a woman meets the objectives, he assumes she loves him. If she fails to meet the objectives, he will assume she does not love him. The man assumes that if the woman loved him she would have tried harder and he always believes his objectives for her are reasonable."

"What objectives?"

"The objectives are different for each man. Men rarely share these objectives because doing so is a recipe for disaster. No woman would tolerate being given a set of goals."

"So what should a guy do if the woman in his life doesn't meet these secret objectives? How can he get her to change?"

"He can't," he replied. "People don't change to meet the objectives of other people. Men can be molded in small ways—clothing and haircuts and manners—because those things are not important to most men. Women can't be changed at all."

"I'm not hearing anything helpful here."

"The best you can hope for in a relationship is to find someone whose flaws are the sort you don't mind. It is futile to look for someone who has no flaws, or someone who is capable of significant change; that sort of person exists only in our imaginations."

"Let's say I find the person whose flaws I don't mind," I said. "The hard part is keeping her. I haven't had much luck in that department."

"A woman needs to be told that you would sacrifice anything for her. A man needs to be told he is being useful. When the man or woman strays from that formula, the other loses trust. When trust is lost, communication falls apart."

"I don't think you need to trust someone to communicate. I can talk to someone I distrust as easily as someone I trust."

"Without trust, you can communicate only trivial things. If you try to communicate something important without a foundation of trust, you will be suspected of having a secret agenda. Your words will be analyzed for hidden meaning and your simple message will be clouded by suspicions."

"I guess I can see that. How can I be more trusted?"

"Lie."

"Now you're kidding, right?" I asked.

"You should lie about your talents and accomplishments, describing your victories in dismissive terms as if they were the result of luck. And you should exaggerate your flaws."

"Why in the world would I want to tell people I was a failure and an idiot? Isn't it better to be honest?"

"Honesty is like food. Both are necessary, but too much of either creates discomfort. When you downplay your accomplishments, you make people feel better about their own accomplishments. It is dishonest, but it is kind."

"This is good stuff. What other tips do you have?"

"You think casual conversation is a waste of time."

"Sure, unless I have something to say. I don't know how people can blab about nothing."

"Your problem is that you view conversation as a way to exchange information," he said.

"That's what it is," I said, thinking I was pointing out the obvious.

"Conversation is more than the sum of the words. It is also a way of signaling the importance of another person by showing your willingness to give that person your rarest resource: time. It is a way of conveying respect. Conversation reminds us that we are part of a greater whole, connected in some way that transcends duty or bloodline or commerce. Conversation can be many things, but it can never be useless."

For the next few hours the old man revealed more of his ingredients for successful social living. Express gratitude. Give more than is expected. Speak optimistically. Touch people. Remember names. Don't confuse flexibility with weakness. Don't judge people by their mistakes; rather, judge them by how they respond to their mistakes. Remember that your physical appearance is for the benefit of others. Attend to your own basic needs first; otherwise you will not be useful to anyone else.

I didn't know if I could incorporate his ingredients into my life, but it seemed possible.

AFFIRMATIONS

"I've heard of something called affirmations," I said, taking the opportunity to spelunk another tunnel in the old man's brain. "You write down your goals fifteen times a day and then somehow they come true as if by magic. I know people who swear by it. Does that really work?"

"The answer is complicated."

"I have time," I said.

"People who use affirmations know what they want and are willing to work for it; otherwise they would not have the enthusiasm to write down their goals fifteen times every day. It should be no surprise that they have more success than the average person."

"Because they work harder?"

"Because they know what they want," he said. "The

ability to work hard and make sacrifices comes naturally to those who know exactly what they want.

"Most people believe they have goals when, in fact, they only have wishes. They might tell you their goal is to get rich without working hard, without making sacrifices or taking risks. That is not a goal, it is a fantasy. Such people are unlikely to write affirmations daily because it would be too much effort. And they are unlikely to be successful in any big way."

"So the affirmations are unnecessary?"

"They have a purpose. Writing your goals every day gives you a higher level of focus. It tunes your mind to better recognize opportunities in your environment."

"What do you mean by tuning your mind?"

"Have you ever had the experience where you hear a strange word for the first time, and then soon afterward you hear the same word again?"

"That happens all the time," I said. "It's freaky. It's as if hearing a word for the first time makes it appear everywhere. Like *fescue*. I never heard of that word until I saw it on a package of grass seed in the store last week. That night I was at a party and some guy used the word. I'm fairly sure I've never heard that word before in my entire life, then I hear it twice in a matter of hours. What are the odds of that?

"And last night I was at my neighbor's house down the street, shooting some pool on his new table. I asked him if he ever played a game called foosball. It's that table game where you use handles connected to little soccer players and try to kick a wooden ball into the other guy's goal."

His face said that he didn't need to know the details of foosball table design.

"Anyway," I continued, "we talked about foosball for twenty minutes, how we both played it in college but hadn't seen a foosball table in years. I can't remember the last time I uttered the word *foosball*. Fifteen minutes later, I'm walking home and something catches my eye in an upstairs window of a neighbor's house. I'll be darned if it wasn't a bunch of kids playing foosball. I've gone past that house a thousand times and never seen that foosball table in the window before."

"Your brain can only process a tiny portion of your environment," he said. "It risks being overwhelmed by the volume of information that bombards you every waking moment. Your brain compensates by filtering out the 99.9 percent of your environment that doesn't matter to you. When you took notice of the word *fescue* for the first time and rolled it around in your head, your mind tuned itself to the word. That's why you heard it again so soon."

"It's still a coincidence. I don't think people are saying *fescue* around me every day."

"Yes, probability is still involved. But *fescue* and *foosball* were only a few of the unusual words and ideas that you tuned your brain to this week. The others didn't cross your path again so you took no notice of their absence. When you consider all of the coincidences that are possible, it is not surprising that you experience a few every day.

"A person who does affirmations takes mental tuning to a higher level. The process of concentrating on the goal every day greatly increases the likelihood of noticing an opportunity in the environment. The coincidence will create the illusion that writing down the goal causes the environment to produce opportunities. But in reality the only thing that changes is the person's ability to notice the opportunities. I don't mean to minimize that advantage because the ability to recognize opportunities is essential to success."

"Well, maybe that's part of it," I said. "But I've heard of some pretty amazing coincidences that happened for the people doing affirmations. One of my friends was writing affirmations to double his income and he got a phone call out of the blue from a headhunter. Two weeks later he's in a new job at double his salary. How do you explain that?"

"Your friend had a clear goal and was willing to make

changes in his life to accomplish it," he responded. "His willingness to do affirmations was a good predictor of his success, not necessarily a cause of it. The headhunter in your example increased the pay of many people that month. Your friend was one of them.

"People who do affirmations will have the sensation that they are causing the environment to conform to their will. This is an immensely enjoyable feeling because the illusion of control is one of the best illusions you can have."

He continued. "Another way to look at affirmations is as a communication channel between your conscious and sub-conscious mind. Your subconscious is often better than your rational mind at predicting your future. If your subconscious allows you to write 'I will be a famous ballerina' fifteen times a day for a year, it's telling you something. Your subcon-scious is saying it likes your odds, that it will allow you to make the sacrifices, that it will give you the satisfaction you need to weather the hard work ahead. On the other hand, if you try writing your affirmation for a few days and find it too bothersome, your subconscious is giving you a clear message that it doesn't like your odds."

"I don't see why my subconscious would be better than my conscious mind at predicting my future. I thought the subconscious was irrational," I said.

"The subconscious is an odds-calculating machine. That's what it does naturally, though not always to good effect. If your subconscious notices that you lost money on your last three business dealings with people who wear hats, you'll never trust people in hats again. Your subconscious isn't always right; it depends on the quality of the information you feed into its odds-calculating engine. Luckily, the topic your subconscious knows best is you, because it has known you since you were in the womb. If your subconscious allows you to spend ten minutes out of every busy day writing, 'I will double my income,' your subconscious likes your odds and it is qualified to make that prediction."

"Couldn't affirmations be more than that?" I asked. "You made a big deal about saying things aren't exactly what they seem, but who's to say that concentrating on your goals doesn't change probability?"

"Go on," he said.

"Okay, imagine you're a sea captain but you're blind and deaf. You shout orders to your crew, but you don't know for sure if they heard the orders or obeyed them. All you know is that when you give an order to sail to a particular warm port, within a few days you are someplace warm. You can never be sure if the crew obeyed you, or took you to some other warm place, or if you went nowhere and the weather improved. If, as you say, our minds are delusion generators, then we're all like blind and deaf sea captains shouting orders into the universe and hoping it makes a difference. We have no way of knowing what really works and what merely seems to work. So doesn't it make sense to try all the things that appear to work even if we can't be sure?"

"You have potential," he said.

I didn't know what that meant.

FIFTH LEVEL

"Who are you?" I asked. I didn't know how to phrase the question politely. The old man certainly wasn't normal.

"I'm an Avatar."

"Is that some sort of title? I thought it was your name."

"It's both."

"Excuse me for asking this. I don't really know how to phrase it, so I'm just going to come out and say it—"

"You want to know if I'm human."

"Yeah. I apologize if that sounds crazy. It's just that . . ."

The old man waved off the end of my sentence.

"I understand. Yes, I am human. I'm a fifth-level human; an Avatar."

"Fifth level?"

"People exist at different levels of awareness. An Avatar is one who lives at the fifth level."

"Is awareness like intelligence?" I asked.

"No. Intelligence is a measure of how well you function within your level of awareness. Your intelligence will stay about the same over your life. Awareness is entirely different from intelligence; awareness involves recognizing your delusions for what they are. Most people's awareness will advance one or two levels in their lifetime."

"What does it mean to recognize your delusions?"

"When you were a child, did your parents tell you that Santa Claus brought presents on Christmas Day?"

"Yeah," I said, "I believed in Santa until kindergarten, when the other kids started talking. Then I realized Santa couldn't get to all those homes in one night."

"Your intelligence did not change at the moment you realized that Santa Claus was a harmless fantasy. Your math and verbal skills stayed the same, but your awareness increased. You were suddenly aware that stories from credible sources—in this case your parents—could be completely made up. And from the moment of that realization, you could never see the world the same way because your awareness of reality changed."

"I guess it did."

"And in school, did you learn that the Native Americans and the Pilgrims got together to celebrate what became Thanksgiving in the United States?"

"Yeah."

"You figured it must be true because it was written in a book and because your teachers said it happened. You were in school for the specific purpose of learning truth; it was reasonable to believe you were getting it. But scholars now tell us that a first Thanksgiving with Pilgrims and Native Americans never happened. Like Santa Claus, much of what we regard as history is simply made up."

"In your examples, there's always learning. That seems like intelligence to me, not awareness."

"Awareness is about *unlearning*. It is the recognition that you don't know as much as you thought you knew."

He described what he called the five levels of awareness and said that all humans experience the first level of awareness at birth. That is when you first become aware that you exist.

In the second level of awareness you understand that other people exist. You believe most of what you are told by authority figures. You accept the belief system in which you are raised.

At the third level of awareness you recognize that humans are often wrong about the things they believe. You feel that you might be wrong about some of your own beliefs but you don't know which ones. Despite your doubts, you still find comfort in your beliefs.

The fourth level is skepticism. You believe the scientific method is the best measure of what is true and you believe you have a good working grasp of truth, thanks to science, your logic, and your senses. You are arrogant when it comes to dealing with people in levels two and three.

The fifth level of awareness is the Avatar. The Avatar understands that the mind is an illusion generator, not a window to reality. The Avatar recognizes science as a belief system, albeit a useful one. An Avatar is aware of God's power as expressed in probability and the inevitable recombination of God consciousness.

"I think I'm a fourth-level," I said, "at least according to you."

"Yes, you are a fourth," he confirmed.

"But now that you've told me all your secrets from the fifth level, maybe I get bumped up a level. Is that how it works?"

"No," he said, "awareness does not come from receiving new information. It comes from rejecting old information. You still cling to your fourth-level delusions."

"I feel vaguely insulted," I joked.

"You shouldn't. There is no implied good or bad about one's level of awareness. No level is better or worse than any other level. People enjoy happiness at every level and they contribute to society at every level."

"That sounds very charitable," I said, "but I notice your level has the highest number. That's obviously the good one. You must be feeling a little bit smug."

"There is no good or bad in anything, just differences in usefulness. People at all levels have the same potential for being useful."

"But you have to feel glad you're not on one of the other levels."

"No. Happiness comes more easily at the other levels. Awareness has its price. An Avatar can find happiness only in serving."

"How do you serve?"

"Sometimes society's delusions get out of balance, and when they conflict, emotions flame out of control. People die. If enough people die, God's recombination is jeopardized. When that happens, the Avatar steps in."

"How?"

"You can't wake yourself from a dream. You need someone who is already awake to shake you gently, to whisper in your ear. In a sense, that is what I do."

"As usual, I'm not sure what you mean."

He explained, "The great leaders in this world are always the least rational among us. They exist at the second level of awareness. Charismatic leaders have a natural ability to bring people into their delusion. They convince people to act against self-interest and pursue the leaders' visions of the greater good. Leaders make citizens go to war to seize land they will never live on and to kill people who have different religions."

"Not all leaders are irrational," I argued.

"The most effective ones are. You don't often see math geniuses or logic professors become great leaders. Logic is a detriment to leadership."

"Well, irrational leadership must work. The world seems to be chugging along fairly well, overall."

"It works because people's delusions are, on average, in balance. The Avatar keeps it so by occasionally introducing new ideas when needed."

"Do you think an idea can change the world that much?" I asked.

"Ideas are the only things that can change the world. The rest is details."

GOING HOME

Time and need dissolved in the old man's presence. We talked for what could have been several days. I remember one sunrise, but there might have been more. I never felt tired in his presence. It was as if energy surrounded him like an invisible field, feeding everything that was near. He was amazing and confounding and, ultimately, beyond the realm of words.

We talked more about life and energy and probability. At times I lost the sense of belonging to my own body. It was as if my consciousness expanded to include items in the room. I stared at my hand as it rested on the arm of the rocking chair and watched as the distinctions between wood and air and hand disappeared. At times I felt like a kitten lifted by the fold of skin on the back of my neck, helpless, safe, transported.

I don't remember leaving his house or walking to my van, but I do remember how everything looked. The city had bright edges. Sound was crisp. Colors were vivid. Objects seemed more dimensional, as if I could see the sides and backs from any angle. I heard a phone call being made a block away and knew both sides of the conversation. I could feel every variation in airflow.

I drove home by a route I wouldn't normally take. I glided through green lights without ever touching my brakes. Pedestrians stayed on sidewalks and a policeman waved me around an accident scene. I knew that all the people involved were safe.

As my key entered the lock, I could see all the other locks like mine and all the other keys that were coincidentally the same. I could see the internal mechanism of the lock as it turned, as though I were a tiny observer inside, looking at industrial-sized equipment.

Everything in my apartment seemed three-quarters of its original size. It was mildly claustrophobic.

I sat down at my kitchen table with the package that the Avatar refused to accept and I stared at it for a while, wondering about its contents. I wanted to open it but didn't want anything to spoil a perfect mood. In time, however, curiosity won.

A folded yellow note tumbled out of the box and into my lap. I unfolded it and read its barely legible message. It was just one sentence, but there was so much in the sentence that I found myself reading it over and over. I stayed up all that night, wrapped in the red plaid blanket that was also in the package, reading the sentence.

"There is only one Avatar at a time."

AFTER THE WAR

"I love that rocking chair," the young man said to me. How old is that thing? It looks like an antique."

"I got it one year before the Religion War," I said.

"I'm glad that war ended before I was born," the young man sighed. "I can't imagine what it was like to be alive then."

"You are lucky to have missed it."

"Were you in that war?"

"Everyone was in that war."

"Let me ask you something," he said. "Why do you think the war ended? We learned in school that everyone just stopped fighting. No one knows why. Although there are all kinds of theories about secret pacts among world leaders, no one really knows. You were there. Why do you think everyone suddenly stopped fighting?"

"Put another log on the fire and I'll tell you."

The young man looked at his watch and hesitated. He had many more stops before lunch. Then he turned toward the fireplace and chose a sturdy log.

"If you flip a coin," I said, "how often does it come up heads?"

THE END

Comments:
scottadams@aol.com